What is There in "Hell" You Want?

An exploration of those who finish this life outside of Christ

Authored by:
Drexel T. Brunson, Ph.D.

Copyright © 2014 Drexel T. Brunson, Ph.D.
All rights reserved.

ISBN: 1500218235
ISBN 13: 9781500218232

ENDORSEMENTS

From the creative pen of a faithful pastor comes a definitive work on a difficult subject – hell. Even for the most devout, the subject is very challenging. Hence you will find a Bible-based treatment, which will bring a balance between the reality of hell and the reality of God's saving grace.

Dr. Richard Dresselhaus
Author, *"The Deacon and His Ministry"*
San Diego, CA

The thought of a person going to an eternal hell, a place of punishment without hope, should make any sane individual recoil at the prospect for himself or any other person. Perhaps that accounts for the reticence of the truth being proclaimed today, but does not make it less true. Drexel Brunson has, with carefulness and gentleness of spirit, presented this reality in a clear and fresh way. He does not base his teaching on any one, possibly disputed, text, but gives a balanced full-Bible presentation that should leave no doubt of the certainty of the reality of hell. The book should be read by every preacher seeking a balanced view of a difficult, but not uncertain, reality.

Pastor Lowell Harrup
Northland Cathedral, Kansas City, MO

With deep spiritual insight, years of personal pastoral experience and a heart for biblical truth, Drexel Brunson brings to "center stage" an almost forgotten certainty that is so needed today. He makes us see the reality of hell and judgment and challenges us to seek the ultimate desire of God – that "none should perish, but that all should come to repentance." (2 Peter 3:9). This work will be an outstanding resource for pastors and teachers.

Dr. John Hedgepeth
Pastor, Northwood Temple, Fayetteville, NC

The difficult subject of "hell" has been handled very well by Dr. Brunson. He has approached the subject in a scholarly manner without making it difficult to follow. This is the best treatment of the subject I have found. Clergy and laity alike will appreciate the development and handling of this extremely important subject.

Pastor Bill Newby
Crown Pointe Church, Lee's Summit, MO

This is a very practical book that will be extremely helpful for pastors, church leaders, and good for all those who would like to be informed of what happens to an individual who concludes life outside of Christ. Having pastured thirty-one years and serving as a college professor for eight years, and having served as a hospital chaplain for one-and-a-half years, these positions teach me that the knowledge derived from this book is critical to use because it warns people to flee the wrath to come.

Gardener Altman, Sr., Master of Divinity
Doctor of Divinity, Fayetteville, NC

DEDICATION

I dedicate this book to my wife, Pamala, who has exemplified for all of our thirty-nine years of marriage the virtuous woman of Proverbs 31. I further dedicate this book to my son, Jarrod, and his wife, Liz (my daughter-in-law), who together exemplify the love Solomon testified of in the Song of Solomon. I thirdly dedicate this book to my daughter, Kellyn, and her husband, Trey (my son-in-law), who exemplify praise to God through song and prayer as did David in Psalm 42:8. Lastly, I dedicate this book to my just-born fraternal twin grandchildren, Quaid (grandson) and Lakely (granddaughter), for whom I pray the Old Testament blessing of Numbers 6:24–26. I love you all!

ACKNOWLEDGMENTS

As with almost any major project, the publication of this book is the product of many people beyond myself. I want to acknowledge their participation in this effort. My wife, Pam, is one to whom I dedicated this book. I acknowledge my gratitude for her patience as I researched, wrote, revised, and edited this volume. She gave me the time to write, and I am forever grateful. The spiritual service that comes from this effort belongs to her, for without her long-suffering graciousness, this volume would not have come into reality but would have remained conceptual.

I am also grateful to April Charland, who with her bountiful skills, has with excellence, patience, and good humor converted the manuscript to typed copy.

I am also grateful to Rev. Warren Bullock, the Executive Presbyter for the Northwest Districts of the Assemblies of God in the United States. He is a man of gentle nature, high character, and theological insight. I am appreciative that he reviewed this book for its theology and correctness in scriptural application. I thank him for writing the foreword for this book.

There is a group of people who are very close to me, and they have each in their own way contributed to the development of this book. Mrs. Sarah Brunson, my mother, and Mrs. Mildred Knight, my aunt, have prayed for me, read the manuscript for errors and overall readability, and have kindly shared their insights, which provided me the opportunity to identify where clarifications were needed. My mother specifically allowed me to draw upon her academic skills as she, at my request, engaged with me in a word-for-word editing process. However, any errors remain mine.

The encouragement of my brothers, Steve Brunson and Phillip Brunson, has been invaluable. They would call and encourage me to continue forward progress on the book. They always had, as the Bible speaks, a word in due season, and it was good (Proverbs 15:23).

I am also grateful for the concern that the much-appreciated former sheriff of Marion County, Ed Dean, has shown to me. He has been a friend, and while he did not participate in the writing of this book, he did allow me to coauthor *"The Servant Organization for Jesus"* with him, which gave me insight on how to publish a book. I also thank his executive assistant, Ms. Terri Judy, for advising April Charland on how to prepare this manuscript for the publishers and other needed pieces of information.

Thank you all for your contribution to this book and my life.
Drexel

TABLE OF CONTENTS

Endorsements	iii
Dedication	v
Acknowledgments	vii
Foreword	xi
Introduction	xiii
Chapter One: The Old Testament: Setting the Stage	1
Chapter Two: Sheol: Disillusionment, Separation, and Punishment	13
Chapter Three: The Epistles of Paul	25
Chapter Four: The Synoptics Plus John	37
Chapter Five: Jesus's Descent into Hell, the Lake of Fire	53
Chapter Six: Hell Is Not Culturally Popular	67
Chapter Seven: What Does It Mean to Be "Inside of Christ" and "Outside of Christ"?	79

Chapter Eight: The Love of God					95

Bibliography					105

Foreword

I was having lunch with a group of colleagues who, like me, were pastors. As most ministers do when they get together, we were talking "church." Part of our discussion centered around the fact that many of the churches we knew about, including some of our own, were not growing. In fact, some of them had not had a single convert in the past year.

After listening to our concerns, the respected pastor of the largest church among us finally spoke up: "Do you want to know why so many churches are not having converts?" Of course we did. He responded, "Because we do not really believe in hell!" There was a long silence, so he went on. "We say we believe in hell. Our doctrine affirms that such a place exists. But if we actually believed it, truly believed it, we would be far more highly motivated to win lost people than we are."

What is There in "Hell" You Want helps to provide that motivation. It is a wake-up call. It is an alarm clock with no snooze button. It is an emergency siren. It points us to the biblical truth we say we believe and calls us to action.

Drexel Brunson leads us carefully through the unfolding of the doctrine of eternal punishment in Scripture. He guides us into the law and prophets, the historical and poetical books, the Gospels and the epistles, and the apocalyptic literature. All contribute to a biblical understanding of hell—its reality, its certainty, and its horror. We are faced with the unvarnished fact that hell is the destiny of those outside of Christ.

If that's all this book was about, it might be motivating, but it could also be depressing. But it is balanced by the grace-filled truth that God is "not wanting anyone to perish, but everyone to come to repentance" (II Peter 3:9). The agape love of Christ that compelled him to offer himself as a substitute for the sinner is a timeless truth strongly emphasized here. One does not need to remain outside of Christ, but can be in Christ. Thus, no hell, no eternal punishment. Instead, heaven! What a glorious prospect!

Caution: this book will irritate some readers. The self-satisfied will find it unsettling. It will challenge the concept of God as a tolerant grandfather who allows most behavior without consequences. It will rouse sleepy Christians from their lethargy and apathy by putting spiritual destinations in clear contrast. The apostle Paul's exhortation speaks to drowsy Christians: "The hour has come for you to wake up from your slumber, because our salvation is nearer now than when we first believed" (Romans 13:11). And if as Christians our salvation is near, the destruction is near for those who do not know our Savior.

Some will split hairs over the author's interpretation of certain Scriptures. Others will resurrect the old, trite argument— "If God is a God of love, he won't send anyone to hell." He *is* a God of love, but the detailed Scriptural evidence for hell outlined in this book is unshakeable. As one person put it, "Hell is real, and lost people are going there."

I was convicted by the truths in this book. As a minister of the Word, I have not preached as much about hell as I have about heaven. Certainly we cannot preach on the subject of eternal damnation as if we are happy that people will go there. However, we can preach it with tears over the lost, but also with hope for the repentant. Jesus still welcomes home the wayward son, the prodigal daughter, the alcoholic father, and the addicted mother. Jesus opens His arms to the rich, moral man, the promiscuous teenager, and the elderly person who has wasted his life. "Everyone who calls on the name of the Lord will be saved" (Romans 10:13).

That is the ultimate message of this book. Forgiveness is available through Jesus Christ our Lord.

Warren D. Bullock
Executive Presbyter, Northwest Region, General Council of the Assemblies of God

Introduction

The writing of this book is the end product of a commitment that I made to my friend, Judson Cornwall, years ago. Serving on the board of a publishing company, Judson invited me to coauthor with him a book detailing a fresh examination of hell. Together we agreed that there has been in recent decades a dearth of preaching and teaching about the eternal place of punishment and separation from God, the final place for all those who are outside of Christ. Unfortunately, for me, Judson went to heaven before I could act on my commitment.

Judson had suggested the title, What in Hell Do you Want? It is an arresting title, very much in the tradition of the shock-type book. I have varied from his title suggestion concerned that it might appear that I am using inappropriate language. I am comfortable that Judson (whose work I use several times in this book) would approve of the altered title, *What is There in Hell You Want?*

I am by choice "in-Christ," but I freely acknowledge that I am an imperfect person. Because I am in-Christ, I have the privilege of carrying in my soul the assurance of the Holy Spirit that heaven will by my eternal home. So when I see Judson, I will be happy to tell him that I kept my word to write the study on hell even though I missed the pleasure of writing with one of the finest Bible teachers that I have ever known.

In my research for this overview volume, I discovered the book *"The Formation of Hell"* authored by Alan Bernstein in 1993 and published by the Cornell University Press. The book is, in my exposure, the finest single-volume detailed examination of this subject that I have thus far reviewed. The ideas were well developed and fresh to my evangelical mindset. His development of thought about hell presented new ways of considering the topic for me. By and large, the evangelical church has not been exposed to many of Dr. Bernstein's ideas, though the evangelical community and he share many agreements.

Dr. Bernstein's book answers the question of "What will happen to the wicked?" in his thirteen-chapter, 392-page book. To write the first five chapters of this overview, I have drawn from many of Dr. Bernstein's ideas and quoted him almost thirty times to answer the question at the conclusion of Chapter Five; "What will happen to those who finish this life outside of Christ?" I am grateful for his book, glad to introduce his thoughts to the evangelical community, and urge all who read this book to acquire Dr. Bernstein's very detailed hardcover, "*The Formation of Hell*" for additional information that I did not include in this volume.

This book is an overview volume; I hope a cursory review of the bibliography will demonstrate is well researched. Very much in the tradition of John Mark, who wrote the shortest Gospel, I have sought to write an approximately one-hundred-page volume so the average reader preparing for a sermon, Sunday school class, home fellowship teaching, academic lecture, or just plain informational reading could know what that place of rejection by God is like. The underlying theme detailing God's love for us and His overpowering desire that people do not select to live in eternity separate from Him runs throughout this overview volume.

I am aware that the topic of hell is not a popular topic in our culture. However, its lack of popularity does nothing to erase its reality. So, to demonstrate the horror of hell, in the first five chapters, I describe the gradual revelation of hell in the Holy Bible to answer the question at the end of chapter 5: "What will happen to those who finish this life outside of Christ?" Chapter one examines Sheol coupled with the hope of Job that there will come a separation in Sheol of the righteous from the unrighteous.

Chapter 2 continues the overview of the gradual revelation of hell by continuing to examine the Old Testament. It will be seen that because of a frustration with the Deuteronomy 28 justice system, the Jewish people were more open to receiving revelation of the postmortem punishment for the unrighteous (in the New Testament, that is defined as those outside of Christ). It will also be seen that there will be a separation in Sheol between the righteous and the unrighteous, and an opaque understanding that there will be punishment for the unrighteous in Sheol emerges. Chapter 3 considers the chronological revelation of hell contained in Paul's epistles, preparing for chapter 4, which considers the revelation of Jesus about hell in the Synoptic Gospels and the Gospel according to John. Chapter 5 describes the descent of Jesus into hell after the crucifixion and hypothesizes what may have occurred in that descent. Additionally, the unique revealing of the lake of fire found only in Revelation is considered. Then chapter 5 ends with the details, based upon the revelations examined in the previous chapters, of "What happens to those who finish this life outside of Christ?"

Chapter 6 examines what I have previously referred to in this introduction—that is, why hell is not a culturally acceptable subject and what the faithful minister and layperson must do about the situation. Chapter 7 explains what it means to be "in Christ" and "outside Christ." Finally, chapter 8 explains that God the Father is a loving God and that He is not willing that any should perish, but He wants all to accept His son Jesus as both Savior and Lord, thus escaping the punishment of hell.

It is my humble hope that this overview book on hell will have the effect of sharpening an evangelistic thrust in our hearts to warn, where it is appropriate, our family, friends, and acquaintances to flee the wrath to come.

I conclude this introduction with a 1947 experience from my personal history that is still spoken about from time to time in my family today. My maternal great-grandfather, whose mother was apparently religious and a member of a Baptist church, was himself a rather spiritually dark individual who had no relationship to Christ but instead gravitated away from the things of the Kingdom of God. He was reported to practice witchcraft, was a noted unbeliever, and ridiculed my maternal grandfather (his son) for going to church and for his belief that people could go to heaven when they died. He arrived at the point of his own death. His sons were in the room; among them was my grandfather, a solid Christian who himself died in 1969. Sadly, my grandfather reported that as part of the deathwatch, his father (my great-grandfather) came into extreme agitation, screaming and imploring his sons to "scare away and shoot" something at the foot of his iron bed. My grandfather interpreted that his father was perceiving demonic spirits, which would at his death, take his soul. This occurred six years prior to my birth but now, six decades into my life, the family, now four generations removed from my great-grandfather's death, has not forgotten the horror of his last moments on earth. I am told that he lived to almost seventy-six years on this earth, a very short time when eternity is contemplated. Without asserting his place in eternity, for that is solely in God's purview, the memory of his departure from this earth has served as a warning to our family to flee the wrath to come.

It may well be that there are other stories that can be told of people in your own family who, in the last few minutes of life, dreaded to meet the Lord and expressed that in some way…I am sorry if that is the case. This book will give an understanding of what the Bible teaches will happen to those who conclude their life outside of Christ.

(Recollections of my great-grandfather's death experience were gleaned from my uncle and cousin and my mother, who received the report of his deathbed experience from various people, but my telling of this tragedy can be sourced back to my grandfather, who was there).

CHAPTER ONE

THE OLD TESTAMENT: SETTING THE STAGE

CHAPTER INTRODUCTION

The Old Testament (Jewish people refer to it as the Hebrew Bible) was composed from about 2000 BCE with the occurrence of the story of a man named Job[1], to the last book to be written—Malachi—by the Jewish prophet Malachi in 400 BCE.[2] The stages of

---

[1] Many believe Moses penned the book of Job. That the book of Job is authentic and inspired is proven in that the ancient Hebrews included it in their canon, a fact that is remarkable since Job was not an Israelite. In addition to references by Ezekiel and James, the book is quoted by the Apostle Paul (Job 5:13, I Cor. 3:19).
According to our oldest traditions among Jewish and Christian scholars, the book was written in Hebrew, the language of Moses. The writer must have been an Israelite, as Moses was, because the Jews "were entrusted with the sacred pronouncements of God," (Rom 3:1,2). Additionally, portions of the prose bear stronger resemblance to the Pentateuch than to any other portion of the Bible. Moses also spent forty years in Midian, not far from Uz (near the land occupied by the Edomites and east of the Promised Land), so he could obtain the detailed information recorded in Job. The book was written by Moses while the Israelites were in the wilderness. (See "How Was the Book of Job Written?," answers.yahoo.comquestion/index?qid=…)

[2] The BCE/CE dating system has been accepted by scholars to provide a common dating system. CE (Common Era) and BCE (Before Common Era) makes it possible for Christian and non-Christian peoples to agree on a date. Otherwise we have both the Hebraic and Islamic dating systems, and that is confusing. (See "Common Era," simple.m.wikipedia.org.)

composition can be "distinguished using differences in terminology, institutional bias, explicit references to outside events, and implicit references from politics and social conditions."[3] The thirty-nine books that make up the Old Testament, written by diverse authors over 1,600 years, do not allow for a single straight line of thought as to what happens to those who are wicked (also known as being "outside of Christ"). However, clarity of thought will come forward about what will happen to the deceased ones who are outside of Christ.

THE TWO CATEGORIES OF PUNISHMENT FROM GOD

"The Jewish people were formed by a series of covenants with God" (Bernstein, p. 135). The covenant between God and His people is one of the central themes of the Bible and is the basis for the establishment, maintenance, and future of the Jewish nation and those later grafted into the Jewish people through the blood of Jesus.

Many people have a controversy about how many covenants there are in the Bible. ("How Many Covenants Are There?," christeternalchristianchurch.com), yet there is universal agreement that God established a covenant with Noah when He said He would never destroy the earth with a flood (Gen. 9:8–17). In Genesis 12:1–3, God's covenant with Abraham begins to unfold when God establishes a special relationship with Abraham and his descendants (which we will later learn comes through the lineage of Isaac; Gen. 17:18–21).[4]

A third universally recognized covenant is the Mosaic covenant, where God obligates Himself to defend the followers and descendants of Israel in return for observing His ordinances. These covenants, however, were bifurcated: the God who would bless and give

---

[3] Alan Bernstein, *The Formation of Hell*, Cornell University Press, Ithaca, NY, p. 133.

[4] This does not fully address the Abrahamic Covenant, nor is it my purpose to fully explicate that covenant. For more complete information on the Abrahamic Covenant, see "The Abrahamic Covenant" by Wayne D. Towner at bibletrack.org, 2004–2008.

reward was also the God who would exact terrible punishments (Bernstein, p. 135, excerpted).

The punishments of God generally run on a dual track: ending of life or long-term suffering. James L. Morrison, in the Internet article "Some Thoughts about the Judgment of God," lists several moments when God ends life:

- Because of man's great wickedness, God destroyed the whole earth by flood, killing all the humans except eight (Gen. 6–9).
- Because of their grievous sin, God destroyed Sodom and Gomorrah and other cities of the plain (18, 19).
- God consumed two of Aaron's sons with fire for making an improper offering at the altar (Lev. 10:1–2).
- When Korah, Dathan, and Abiram rebelled against God's anointed leader, Moses, God caused the earth to swallow up them, their households, and their possessions (Num. 16).
- The "Fire of God" consumed one hundred Israelite soldiers who sought to arrest God's prophet Elijah (II Kings 1).
- When the Assyrians, under Sennacherib's leadership in 701 BCE, laid siege to Jerusalem, God in one night brought death to 185,000 Assyrian troops (II Kings 18–19).

(James Morrison, "Some Thoughts about the Judgment of God," Scripture Insights.com. The part about the death of the Assyrian troops is not a part of Mr. Morrison's article.)

However, God would make provision for the righteous. Greg Johnson in his 2006 article, "God Rescues the Righteous," lists for his readers several rescues the Lord has made:

- God rescued Noah (Gen. 6:5–8:19).
- God rescued Lot (Gen. 19:1–29).
- In Psalm 34.4, David proclaims that God rescued him from all of his fears and that the Angel of the Lord encamps around those who fear Him, and He delivers them. (Greg Johnson, "God Rescues the Righteous," lovinggodfellowship.org).

In addition to ending life, the Bible also presents another method of punishment: long-term suffering. "The most prominent example is the consequence of disobedience in Eden. Thenceforth, women must bear children in pain…Men must earn their livelihood by working the ground…these effects will last as long as humanity itself."[5]

Another example can be cited to illustrate that long-term suffering is also used by God to bring punishment: the Tower of Babel. Humankind did not want to be scattered. So, in unity, human beings chose to strengthen their unity by building a tower to bring them to God instead of following God with faith proved by obedience. Seeing their diversion from serving Him, God "scattered them abroad from there over the face of the earth" (Gen. 11:4, 8, 9). There is no end set to the scattering brought about by God changing their language. It will last as long as humanity endures.[6]

Punishment by the destruction of life does not do away with punishment after death, which germinates from the understanding that one of God's judgments is long-term suffering.

A HUMAN HAS A SOUL, AND THAT SOUL DOES NOT DIE

Dr. James Tabor, in his Internet article "What the Bible Says about Death, Afterlife, and the Future" (Clas-pages.uncc.edu), writes "The Ancient Hebrews had no idea of an immortal soul living a full and vital existence beyond death…Human beings, like the beasts of the field, are made of the 'dust of the earth' and at death they return to that dust." (Gen. 2:7, 3:19). For all practical purposes, death was the end. However, while that may be generally true, we do see the clear development in the Old Testament that we have a soul, and it continues to live on after the death of the body.

- Job 14:13, 14—Two thousand years BCE, Job anticipates descent into Sheol.

---

5 Bernstein, p. 135.

6 Bernstein, p. 136. My gratitude to Alan Bernstein is acknowledged. His outline has been used to address the issues of this chapter in which the duality of God's punishment is addressed.

- Deuteronomy 18:9–13—God directly forbids contact (calling up) the dead.[7]
- I Samuel 28—The necromancer at Endor calls Samuel back from death for the disguised king Saul. (The Hebrew words for "medium" and "necromancer" in Deuteronomy 18 are the same words used in I Samuel 28:9 to describe the occupation in which this woman is illegally engaging.) When the spirit arose, the necromancer said she saw *elohim*, "gods" (but not the God). By this, she meant another worldly or transcendental being, rather than a god.[8]

It is absolutely clear that this is Samuel. He has Samuel's memory, but that, in and of itself, is not proof that it was Samuel. Necromancers, perhaps ignorantly but nevertheless generally, contact demonic spirits who have their own memories of the dead person's activities and will pose as the dead person in order to draw those the necromancer is serving deeper into the will of Satan. What proves that this spirit who rose out of the ground was really Samuel was the fact that he accurately predicted Saul's death in the next battle, which would occur on Mount Gilboa the next day. (See I Sam. 28:15–19.) Demons cannot predict the future.

It is absolutely clear, from the raising of Samuel, that the Old Testament teaching that humans have a soul and that the soul lives on after physical death is true. The soul does not reside on the face of the earth. It may have been a small emerging understanding, but the teaching that humans have a soul in the Old Testament is indisputable.

---

7 God will not give misdirection. If it were impossible to contact the living souls of the dead, God would not have had to forbid it. But our soul is alive after the body dies. And contact is forbidden. See also Lev. 19:31; Lev. 20:6, NET; Isa. 8:19, NIV.

8 Bernstein, p. 138. Bernstein cited Fredrich Netscher, Altorientelischer und altestamexilixher Auferstehungsglaben (1926; rpt, Darmstadt: Wissenschaftliche Buchgesellschaft, 1980), 209 n. I.

SHEOL: THE ABODE OF THE DEAD

Saul's summons disturbed Samuel, and he (Samuel) comes up from out of the earth (I Sam. 28:13). Samuel has been in Sheol, below.

Before we examine Sheol in some detail, it is important to note that it is the place where all the dead are contained, good and evil alike. When Samuel prophesies to Saul of his impending death, Samuel says: "Tomorrow you and your sons shall be with me" (I Sam. 28:19). Thus, Saul and his sons will join Samuel below, in the world of the dead, in Sheol. Sheol contains both the righteous and the wicked.[9]

James Orr, in the article "Sheol" in the International Standard Biblical Encyclopedia, explains that in the King James Version, "Sheol" is often translated as "grave" (Gen. 37:35; I Sam. 2:6; Job 7:9; 14:13 ; Ps. 6:5 ; 49:14 ; Isa. 14:11, etc.), or "hell" (e. g., Deut. 32:22; Ps. 9:17, 18:5; Isa. 14:9; Am. 9:2, etc.); and in three places, "pit" (Num. 16:30, 33; Job 17:16). According to Orr, Sheol really means "the unseen world...the abode of the dead."[10] It is down beneath the earth. We see this used in Psalm 30:3, "O Lord, thou has brought up my soul from Sheol, restored me to life from among those gone down to the pit." Not only are we informed in this passage and others that Sheol is down, but we are also informed that it is the soul of the person that descends into Sheol.

Therefore, we see that Scripture is building precept upon precept: humans have eternal souls and at death, the soul descends into Sheol, both the righteous and the unrighteous.

FOUR FACTS THAT AFFIRM SHEOL'S REALITY

1. **It was firmly regarded as the abode of the dead** even though the noun "sheol" has been applied to various matters relating to life (grave, near death).

---

9 Bernstein, p. 139.

10 James Orr, "Sheol," *International Standard Biblical Encyclopedia*, Grand Rapids, MI, 1980, p. 2761. For more information on Sheol, see this well-developed article.

In Sheol, physical life has ended on the earth, and the soul of the dead descends into the underworld below the earth, where they are gathered into tribes and families. This explains the recurring expressions "to be gathered to one's people" and "to go to one's fathers" (Gen. 15:15, 25:8, 17, 49:33; Num. 20:24, 28, 31:2; Dt. 32:50, 34:5).

It is the antithesis of the living condition and the synonym for everything that is gloomy, inert, and insubstantial (Job 26:5; Prov. 2:18, 21:16; Isa. 14:9, 26:14) (Orr, p. 276).

2. **Those in Sheol are conscious**. Though Samuel acknowledged that he was disturbed when he arose out of the earth, he had memory, awareness, emotion, and knowledge of the future (I Sam. 28). Approximately two hundred years later, the prophet Isaiah confirms that those in Sheol have consciousness.

Isaiah, 170-plus years prior to Babylon taking Judah into captivity, uttered a prophetic revelation of the King of Babylon entering Sheol. Isaiah shows us that the souls in Sheol have consciousness: "Sheol, from beneath, is excited over you to meet you when you come. It arouses for you in the spirits of the dead… They will respond and say to you, even you have been made weak as we. You have become like us" (Isa. 14:9–10).

Clearly, those in Sheol have consciousness and awareness. This world beyond the grave is not a place of unconsciousness or lack of awareness. The inhabitants have strong and lonely memories of the world above. According to James Orr, necromancy rests on the idea that there is some communication between the world above and the world below.[11] For that communication to occur in Sheol, they have to have consciousness and awareness.

3. **God has jurisdiction in Sheol.** While it is true and accurate to understand that those in Sheol are separated from those living on the face of the earth, it is also true and accurate to understand that Sheol is not separated from the rule of God. To further illustrate the will of God in Sheol, we turn to the vision of Amos

---

11 Orr, p. 2761.

where he sees God declaring the final ruin of Israel. This is very instructive as to the absolute omnipresence of God; there is no place to hide. Speaking of Israel, God says:

> They will not have a fugitive who will flee or a refugee who will escape, though they dig into Sheol. From there will my hand take them and though they ascend to Heaven, from there I will bring them down. (Amos 9:1–2)

God is the absolute ruler and potentate of all that there is: above the earth, on the earth, and below the earth. "God rules the universe from its farthest limits to its innermost recesses…"[12] Sheol is submitted to the rule of God.

4. **Sheol is used as a metaphor, but it is a place that is below the earth.** This is illustrated by the story of the insurrection of Korah. Moses had announced that only Aaron and the descendants of Aaron would possess the priesthood (Num. 3, cf. Lev. 10:8–15). This announcement brought to light an insidious insurrection surrounding three coconspirators: Korah, Dathan and Abiram.

Three months after the nation of Israel left Egypt, God led them to Mount Sinai in the wilderness of the Sinai Peninsula (Ex. 19:1). In Sinai, the Lord designated that only Aaron, of the tribe of Levi, and his sons would serve as Israel's priests (Ex. 28:1). The remaining Levites were set apart as Aaron's assistants to help him in the work of the tabernacle (Num. 3:5–10). One of the priests was specially designated as the high priest, who would offer the special "most holy" sacrifice on behalf of the people. This most holy sacrifice was to be performed only once a year on Yom Kippur (the Day of Atonement), the tenth day of the seventh month of Tishvi (September–October) (Lev. 23:26–32). It was to atone for all of the

---

12 Bernstein, p. 144-145.

sins of the entire Israelite nation (Lev. 16:34).[13] The pronouncement that the priesthood would rest with Aaron and his descendants was the catalyst for a leadership challenge that apparently had been brewing. Numbers 16 records the most serious rebellion Moses had to face in the forty years in the wilderness wandering. Jude 11 holds Korah responsible for this very serious insurrection, while Numbers 16 lists three coconspirators: Korah, Dathan, and Abiram. It seems that Korah challenged Moses and Aaron's ecclesiastical leadership, while Dathan and Abiram challenged Moses's civil authority. Dathan and Abiram seemed unconcerned over the ecclesiastical leadership; they even refused to come to the tabernacle to speak with Moses there (Num. 16:12).[14]

Korah realized that his single voice would not be sufficient to bring about change. So, Korah clandestinely and systematically succeeded in gathering 250 leaders of the congregation to his cause. The Bible calls them "famous in the congregation, men of renown" (Num. 16:2). Then, their followers came out with incense in their censers to show that their offerings were acceptable also. "Korah assembled all the congregation against Moses and Aaron at the doorway of the tent of meeting" (Num. 16:19). The congregation has been invited to revolt. Such a serious rebellion could only be resolved by the Lord God.

---

13 "The Aaronic Priesthood—a Biblical Analysis" (help4idrs.com/pwtu/PWTUChap14.pdf).

14 Judson Cornwall, *Incense and Insurrection*, Destiny Image Publishers Inc., Shippensburg, PA 1995, pp. 149-151. Korah showed great leadership ability. He had the insurrection well planned and well organized. All he had to do was stand back and let others do the dirty work in the rebellion while he waited in the wings to assume ecclesiastical leadership. Korah was a cousin of Moses. He belonged to the same Kohathite as Moses and Aaron. Additionally, Korah's father, Izhar, was the elder brother of Amram, Moses's father (see Ex. 6:18). Perhaps it was difficult for Korah to respect Moses's position in leadership: "Familiarity breeds contempt." (Excerpted from pp. 149-150).

Korah and his followers sought the priesthood because they believed it to be the common right of all Israelites. Not content to serve on the team as a Levite associate of Aaron, Korah wanted to replace Aaron. What a valuable helper Korah might have been. Perhaps he could have become next in place to Joshua. Instead, Korah led the life of a conspirator, and God dealt with his conspiracy.[15] God let these antagonists bring the entire congregation to the door of the tabernacle, then He appeared (Num. 16:19). Immediately God called for a separation of Moses and Aaron from the entire congregation because He was going to consume the congregation (Num. 16:21). Moses interceded with God for the people, but God replied, "Speak to the congregation, saying, 'get back from around the dwellings of Korah, Dathan, and Abiram'" (Num. 16:24, NASB). Apparently, the three immediately went to their tents when the glory of the Lord appeared, for the glory of the Lord always produces a separation between the true and the false.

Moses led the congregation to the tents of Dathan and Abiram and prophetically said: "By this you shall know that the Lord has sent me...for this is not my doing. If those men die the death of all men, then the Lord has not sent me. But if...the ground opens its mouth and swallows them up with all that is theirs, and they descend alive into Sheol, then you will understand that these men have spurned the Lord" (Num. 16:28–30, NASB). The ground immediately opened and swallowed the leaders, taking them to a place; the place is Sheol.

---

15 Cornwall, *Incense and Insurrection*, pp. 173-176.

"So they and all that belong to them went down alive to Sheol. And the earth closed over them and they perished from the midst of the assembly" (Num. 16:33, NASB).[16]

Sheol is a place. The noun is used metaphorically, but it is first and foremost a place.

ISRAEL ESPOUSED AND HOPED FOR JUSTICE

When writing on the subject of hell and the growing understanding the Hebrews had of the punishment of the wicked, it is important to understand that there existed in Israel's culture the expectation of justice.

The Ten Commandments probably is the best known portrayal of the Old Testament law (the Torah/Pentateuch), but in the traditional Jewish view, the Torah (the first five books of the Bible) in its entirety constitutes the law. In his closing words to the congregation shortly before he climbs Mount Nebo and is taken to heaven, Moses tells the congregation of Israel:

---

16 Ibid., pp. 174-176. The punishment of the three conspirators was severe. The verses in Num. 16:32, 33 declare that Dathan's and Abiram's wives and children, who stood with them, fell into the opened earth. However, it appears that Korah went into Sheol alone; apparently his family did not join him in the insurrection. Korah must have been standing by himself in front of Dathan and Abiram's tents, for he was a Levite and his tent would have been in the area of the Tabernacle.

Sovereign grace spared the sons of Korah from the fate of their father. Later the sons of Korah, with their sons, became the keepers of the gates of the Tabernacle. They were overseers of the treasures of the house of the Lord and the instruments of the sanctuary; therein, oil and other commodities were in their charge. They were mighty men of valor, strong men who became the royal guards for kings. The Holy Spirit also inspired the sons of Korah to write many of the Psalms. God extended grace to his lineage (see Ps. 84, credited to the sons of Korah). This note is excerpted from pp. 174-177 of Cornwall, *Incense and Insurrection*.

"I command you today to love the Lord your God, to walk in His ways and to keep His commandments and His statues and His judgments, that you may live and multiply, and that the Lord your God may bless you in the land where you are entering to possess it. But if your heart turns away, and you will not obey, but are drawn away and worship other gods and serve them, I declare to you today that you shall surely perish. You will not prolong your days in the land where you are crossing the Jordan to enter and possess it."(Deuteronomy 30:16–18, NASB)

So the Deuteronomic code was "obey and prosper, turn away and perish." This was not only the direction for the nation, but it also applied to the individual. The perceived condition of the individual, or nation, was viewed in the light of Moses's address. A person is rewarded for obedience and cursed for disobedience. Israel lived in a culture that anticipated justice.

Chapter Summary

The stage has been set for a biblical clarity to emerge about what happens to the wicked (those outside of Christ) after their life is concluded on earth. The Hebrews understood that God would judge, and His judgment would occur by destruction of life and/or long-term suffering. This lays the groundwork for an eternal future of long-term suffering for the wicked dead.

The Hebrews also understood that there is an abode for the dead, and in this abode the soul of the righteous and the wicked reside. The abode is below the earth, and the abode's name is Sheol.

The Hebrews understood that those in Sheol were not asleep but fully conscious and aware. There was no doubt in the mind of the Hebrews that God has complete and absolute jurisdiction in Sheol. For the Hebrew mind and heart, Sheol was used as a metaphor for death and the grave, but it is first and foremost the abode of the dead.

Chapter Two

Sheol: Disillusionment, Separation, and Punishment

Chapter Introduction

In chapter 1, the groundwork was established to consider the question, what will happen to the wicked (those outside of Christ)? Considerations of spiritual matters relating to the soul will be addressed in subsequent chapters, but this second chapter will continue to investigate the developing revelations about Sheol and other matters, which brings the answer closer to the question: What will happen to those outside of Christ (also called the wicked, unrighteous, and unbelievers)?

The core revelation of justice in the Old Testament is given in Deuteronomy 28 (the Deuteronomic System). It consists of blessings and punishments in relationship to a nation or individual's self-chosen position before God: blessings for a right relationship, punishment if God is rejected. "These punishments frequently entailed remarkable suffering—famine, plague, defeat, captivity—prior to early, if not ignominious death."[17] After death, however, the wicked and the good alike descended into a vast receptacle called Sheol (the abode of the dead).

In this chapter, the revelation that Sheol does distinguish between the wicked and the righteous will be examined. The additional name of

---

17 Bernstein, p. 154.

Gehenna will be investigated, and finally, the disclosure that judgment and shame are present in Sheol will be discussed.

Disillusionment with Deuteronomic Justice

The first stimulus to better understand what would come to be called "hell" was the people's dissatisfaction with the Deuteronomic justice system. It just took too long for God to enact His judgment, as laid out in Deuteronomy 28, if it ever came at all. The Jewish community was disillusioned.

Asaph, a tenth-century BCE Levite, who served as King David's music director, wrote Psalm 73. He struggled with the prosperity of the wicked:

> …my feet came close to stumbling.
> My steps had almost slipped.
> For I was envious of the arrogant
> As I saw the prosperity of the wicked…
> They are not in trouble as other men
> Nor are they plagued like mankind…
> Behold, these are the wicked
> And always at ease, they have increased in wealth.
> Surely in vain I have kept my heart pure. (Ps. 73:2, 3, 5, 12, 13, NASB).

Asaph will recover his Deuteronomic faith by writing in verse 28: "…the nearness of God is my good; I have made the Lord God my refuge, that I may tell of all your works." However, the importance of this Psalm is to point out the frustration that even strong, mature believers experienced about God waiting too long to affect His judgment on evildoers.

King Solomon, the author of Ecclesiastes, also saw the same conundrum—the righteous suffering and the wicked being blessed. Solomon wrote:

There is a futility which is done on the earth, this is, there are righteous men to whom it happens according to the deeds of the wicked. On the other hand, there are evil men to whom it happens according to the deeds of the righteous. I say that this too is futility. (Ecc. 8:14, NASB)

In the final book of the Old Testament, the prophet Malachi calls attention to the disillusionment of the Jewish community about Deuteronomic justice. God has heard what the Jewish nation is saying:

Your words have been arrogant against me, says the Lord. Yet you say, "what have we spoken against you?" You said, "It is vain to serve God, and what profit is it that we have kept His charge…so we now call the arrogant blessed; not only are doers of wickedness built up but they also test God and escape." (Mal. 3:13–15, NASB)

From these examples, it seemed to the nation of Israel that God waited so long to visit judgment on the wicked that the nation had grown into a frustration over divine justice. That frustration will lead to a greater revelation of what happens to the wicked after death.

Separation within Sheol

The division between the righteous and the wicked begins with Job. The initial call for a division occurs in the book of Job, the oldest historical composition in the Bible (composed orally ca. 2000 BCE). In the account, the plot is exposed when in chapter 1, the Lord reveals Job's righteousness at a time when the sons of God came to present themselves before the Lord and Satan was with them (Job 1:6–8). Satan challenges what will six hundred years later be the Deuteronomic System (ca. 1450 BCE) by asking God to remove the rewards for relationship and obedience to God. Satan's argument is simple: "Remove the rewards and Job will not serve the Lord because he will lose his motivation."

God gave Satan permission to test Job's righteousness by afflicting him with hardship. Satan tries Job; he even imposes some of the Deuteronomy 28 curses by removing his flocks, and his children, and then Job is afflicted with boils. In the end, God affirms Job's right standing with Himself and chastises Job's three friends for saying that he was being punished for his sins. God does not address Elihu, the fourth friend. So the four friends are arguing from the viewpoint of what will later be written by Moses and called the Deuteronomic justice system, and, in this case, they are wrong.[18]

Though Moses reported the suffering of Job six hundred years after Job's anguish, the situation of Job is a challenge to the future Deuteronomy 28 justice system: the innocent Job suffers while the wicked prosper. That is an issue for Job, and he wishes he could hide from God in Sheol, but Job also wants to confront God and argue that he is being undeservedly treated (Job 16:21).

However, in his suffering Job does not envy the wicked who are being blessed. Nor does he hope for their sudden destruction, but he does look for a time when all will be made right. The preeminent injustice for Job is that all the living experience the same death, whether righteous or wicked (Job 21:23–26), and Job, like Solomon, one thousand years later in Ecclesiastes, recognizes the lack of distinction in death. The righteous and the wicked should be distinguished from each other.[19]

Job affirms that God rules Sheol. Job says, "Sheol is naked before Him and destruction has no covering" (Job 26:6). So, surely God can treat the wicked in death differently than the righteous.

Job is challenging the belief about the nature of death at the time he lived (ca. 2000 BCE). At that time, Job's statements create the hypothesis that the dead existed alike in Sheol. Job's own statements support that hypothesis. In Job 7:9 Job imagines that Sheol is characterized by

---

18 Bernstein, pp. 154-157.

19 Bernstein, p. 158. John F. Hartley takes the same view of Job in *The Book of Job*, New International Commentary on the Old Testament, ed. R. K. Harrison (Grand Rapids, MI: Eerdmaus, 1988).

a sameness: "When the cloud vanishes, it (life) is gone. So he who goes down to Sheol, does not come up." Job says nothing about any variance in the way souls are treated. He only states that the soul goes down to Sheol, and it will not come back up. In Job 10:20–22, Job gives us further insight into what his era thought Sheol was like: "…withdraw from me that I may have a little cheer before I go. And I shall not return—to the land of darkness and deep shadow, the hand of utter gloom as darkness itself, of deep shadow without order, and which shines as the darkness."

In an earlier passage, Job thinks of the mixed situation that awaits him and all people in Sheol. In Job 3:14–19, he acknowledges that the wicked, the prisoner, the taskmaster, the small and the great, and the slave are there. There is a mixture of good and evil in Sheol. Job, who longs for the afterlife in Sheol to be different from what he has experienced on earth, wants there to be a distinction between the good and the evil in Sheol (the abode of the dead).[20]

In Psalm 49, one thousand years after Job's distress, the sons of Korah plainly state that the misguided achievements of the worldly will not spare them death, and they will still descend into Sheol, where the upright will rule over them.

> …Those who trust in wealth and boast in the abundance of their riches?…
> As sheep they are appointed to Sheol; death shall be their shepherd;
> And the upright shall rule over them in the morning.
> And their form shall be for Sheol to consume
> So that they have no habitation. (Psalm 49:6, 14, NASB).

However, the sons of Korah see a different future for the righteous in Psalm 49:15: "But God will redeem my soul from the power of Sheol for He will receive me."

The mechanics of redemption are not clear, and rest in faith and hope, but the point remains that the echo of the call for a distinction

---

20 R. R. Friedman, "Evil and Moral Agency," 24(1989):3–30, cited by Bernstein, p. 161.

between the righteous and the wicked first seen in Job is more plainly accepted as fact by the time Psalm 49 is composed (a thousand years after Job's confliction). This lays the groundwork for the distinctions that will later be made in the New Testament about the afterlife of the righteous and the wicked.

Job wanted there to be a distinction between the righteous and the wicked in Sheol, where all the dead go. The sons of Korah assure us in Psalm 49 that the righteous and the wicked are divided but offer no insight into how this occurs. Now, the book of Ezekiel (composed 598–586 BCE) shows us definitively, through a prophesy, that there is a distinction in Sheol between the righteous and the wicked.

In Ezekiel 32, the prophet predicts the fall of the Pharaoh, King of Egypt, using the figure of an animal of prey, such as a lion or crocodile, which is caught, slain, and left as prey for fowl and wild animals. Then Ezekiel says that Babylon will overcome Egypt and the ensuing desolation will be so severe that the rivers will flow as smooth as oil, without any disturbance from man or beast.

The Egyptians, including the Pharaoh, have been defeated and slain and have gone to their grave uncircumcised (died in their sins); thus there will be no resurrection to eternal life. As Pharaoh and his dead troops arrive in Sheol, souls rise to greet them on their entry. Pharaoh and his troops are shown their place among the uncircumcised (32; 22–32). Ezekiel 32:24 teaches that there is more than one fate after death. The wicked suffer agony in the deepest recesses of Sheol. Shame in death is the beginning of hell.

THE PUNISHMENT OF THE WICKED EMERGES

In the book of Psalms, Psalm 11 and Psalm 140 employ the idea of punishment being fiery for the wicked. In Psalm 11, David, who some argue composed this Psalm while in the wilderness of Ziph, contrasts the righteous with the wicked. David is being pursued by Saul; he has been betrayed by the Ziphites, and friends are encouraging him to flee. In that circumstance, it is supposed by some that David wrote this Psalm, whose leading idea is that when our affairs seem to be hopeless, we are not to be in despair, but are to put our trust in God (II Sam. 24–26:2). In the context of the Psalm, David contrasts the righteous with the wicked.[21] The wicked will know the punishment of Sodom and Gomorrah, but the righteous will see the Lord:

> The Lord tests the righteous and the wicked
> And the one who loves violence, his soul hates
> Upon the wicked He will rain snares:
> Fire and brimstone and burning wind
> will be the portion of their cup. (Psalm 11:5–6, NASB)

In Psalm 140, David is in bitter conflict with vicious and unscrupulous men, and he asks God to deliver him from evil men. He applies the pattern of fiery punishment for the wicked and the righteous will dwell in His presence.

> Rescue me, O Lord, from evil men;
> Preserve me from violent men…
> May burning coals fall upon them;
> May they be cast into the fire,
> Into deep pits from which they cannot rise…
> Surely the righteous will give thanks to your name;
> The upright will dwell in your presence. (Ps. 140:1, 10, 13)

The revelation of the punishment of the wicked continues in Isaiah 66, where the prophet is glancing at Israel after their return from Babylon.[22] Isaiah prophesizes the restoration of the temple worship and that as worshippers leave the temple, they would see the dead bodies of those who refused to obey God. The situation of those dead bodies is

---

21 Psalm 11, Barnes Notes, bibleapps.com.
22 "Isaiah Chapter 66," Barnes Notes, sacred-texts.com.

that the fire burns them, and worms that will never die eat them (Isa. 66:24).

Clearly, Israel has an understanding that Sheol (the abode of the dead) treats the wicked dead and the righteous dead differently. Of the wicked dead, a picture of suffering that is equated to eternal fire and undying worms is emerging.

However, though, a revelation of punishment is emerging, Sheol is the place of departed spirits, irrespective of whether a soul is righteous or wicked, but Sheol is not hell. To understand that, we look to the translation of the word *Sheol* in the Old Testament, in the KJV:[23]

- It is translated as "hell" thirty-one times (Deut. 32:22; I Sam. 22:6; Job 1:1–8, 26:6; Psalm 9:17, 16:10, 18:5, 55:15, 86:13, 116:3, 139:8; Prov. 5:5, 7:27, 9:18, 15:11, 15:24, 23:14, 27:20, ISA 5:14, 14:9, 14:15, 28:15, 18, 57:9; Ezk. 31:16, 31:17, 32:21, 32:27; Amos 9:2; Jonah 2:2; Habb. 2:5).
- It is translated as "grave" thirty-one times (Gen. 37:35, 42:38, 44:29, 31; I Sam. 2:6; I Kings 2:6, 9; Job 7:9, 14:13, 17:13, 21:13, 24:19; Psalm 6:5, 30:3, 31:37, 49:14, 15, 83:3, 48, 141:7; Prov. 1:12, 30:16; Eccl. 9:10; SS 8:6; Isa. 14:11, 38:10, 38:18; Ezk. 31:15; Hosea 13:14).
- It is translated as "pit" three times (Num. 16:30, 33; Job 17:16).

But actually, the Hebrew word *Sheol* does not mean any of these three words (hell, grave, or pit). Strong's Hebrew & Chaldee Dictionary says that *Sheol* is "the unseen state." Smith's Bible Dictionary says that "Sheol is always the abode of the departed spirits." Fausset's Bible Dictionary and Encyclopedia says that "Sheol is the common receptacle of the dead."[24]

It is clear that Sheol is not hell, but it is the place of departed spirits. Yet there is a word that emerges to emphasize that there is place of punishment, of burning in an area, a compartment of Sheol. That world is "Gehenna." The word *Gehenna* is of Hebrew origin, originating from

---

23 "Hell, Sheol, Hades, Gehenna, and Tartarus Explained," Liberty University Online, www.scribd.com/doc/22685585, pg. 1.

24 "Charts for Sheol, Hades, Gehenna, and Tartarus," www.what-the-hell.com/hell-study.hellcharts.htm.

the ravine just outside the walls of Jerusalem, beyond the Potsherd Gate (Jer. 19:2) called Ge-Hinnom, named after the Valley of Hinnom or the Valley of the Son of Hinnom (Neh. 11:30; Joshua 15:8).[25] "The translators of the Hebrew Bible into the Greek Septuagint transliterated this name as Gehenna. Early Greek-speaking Christians used the Septuagint as their Bible and later as the Old Testament, so they preserved this term." [26]

"'Gehenna' or the 'Gehenna of Fire' is the Greek word that actually means hell. It is never translated by any other word but hell, and ten of the eleven times the word is used, it is used by the Lord Jesus Christ Himself" [27] with the eleventh time being James, his half brother (Mt. 5:22, 5:29, 30, 10:28, 18:9, 23:15, 23:23; Mk. 9:43, 9:45, 47; Lk. 12:5; Jas. 3:6). Gehenna then is the place that is seen in Sheol as being the place of burning punishment. This is not clear in the Old Testament, but because of Jesus's teachings in the New Testament, a clarity forms.

Sheol then is the abode of the dead, but it is the addition of Gehenna in the New Testament that helps us see that Sheol, though not clear in the Old Testament, does contain a place of punishment, and that place is Gehenna.

Resurrection from Sheol

"Although later Jewish literature would consider the subject in great detail, the Hebrew scriptures speak very little of resurrection. Further,

---

25 The Valley of Hinnom was the place where Ahaz introduced the worship of fire gods, the sun, Baal, and Moloch. Under Manasseh, the Judean population offered their children as burnt offerings to false gods (Jer. 7:31). This cruel worship was finally abolished, and Josiah made the place a receptacle of dead carcasses and bodies of criminals, in which worms would flourish continually. A perpetual fire was kept to consume the putrefying matter. The place was still in existence at the time of Christ, and Jesus illustrated the conditions in Gehenna (hell) by referring to the Hinnom Valley. ("Hell, Sheol, Hades, Gehenna, and Tartarus Explained," pg. 2).

26 Bernstein, pg. 167.

27 "Hell, Sheol, Hades, Gehenna, and Tartarus Explained," pg. 2.

when the subject is addressed in the Hebrew Bible, it is not always in the context of postmortem judgment."[28]

Ezekiel 37 speaks of the resurrection theme, but it does not address a resurrection from Sheol. In Ezekiel 36, the prophet announces that Israel will be restored. Ezekiel 37 illustrates the promise of Ezekiel 36, through the vision of the Valley of Dry Bones (see Ezekiel 37:1–14). "The scattered exiles of both Israel and Judah would be released from the 'graves' of captivity and one day re-gathered in their homeland with the Messiah as their leader. Ezekiel felt as if he was speaking to the dead as he preached to the exiles. But one day God will bring to life the dead bones, he will bring to life (resurrect) a spiritually dead people."[29]

However, Daniel foretold of the resurrection that explicitly includes the wicked. Both the wicked and the righteous are raised from the dead and separated and are surrendered to an eternal future. This picture is the clearest in the Old Testament about the resurrection of the dead out of Sheol (Dan. 12). Daniel definitely informs us that all inhabitants of Sheol, whether righteous or wicked, will be resurrected.

Eternal Punishment

The vision of Daniel envisions two futures: everlasting life and everlasting contempt.

Many of those who sleep in the dust of the ground will awake… to everlasting life, but the other to disgrace and everlasting contempt. (Dan. 12:2, NASB)

"This is a clear reference to the resurrection of both the righteous and the wicked, although the eternal destiny of each will be quite different. Up to this point in time, teaching about the resurrection was not

---

28 Bernstein, p. 171.

29 *Life Application Study Bible*, Tynchle House Publishers Inc., Wheaton, IL, 1996, pg. 1245, footnote on 37:1FF.

common, although every Israelite believed that one day he or she would be included in the restoration of the new kingdom. The reference to a bodily resurrection of both the saved [the righteous] and the lost [the unrighteous] was a sharp departure from common belief."[30]

Chapter Conclusion

This chapter has examined the growth of the revelation of Sheol. Disillusionment over the Deuteronomic justice system was a primary cause for the people's hearts to be open to a revelation of what happens to the wicked.

The chapter also investigated the fact that there is a separation in Sheol between the righteous and the wicked. And the revelation of a "fiery punishment," where worms do not die, was also examined. Finally, Daniel reveals that there will be a resurrection from the dead (those in Sheol), where an eternal future becomes a reality: the righteous will be blessed, and the unrighteous will be cursed.

It has taken approximately 1,600 years of revelation (Job–Malachi) to understand this much about what will happen to the wicked. The attention now turns to Jesus and the writers of the New Testament to further the revelation of what will happen to the wicked.

---

30 Ibid., p. 1288, footnote 12:1.

Chapter Three

The Epistles of Paul

Chapter Introduction

The spotlight of Christianity focuses on everlasting life with Father God, thus achieving the goal God had at the very beginning with Adam and Eve: dwelling together. Although they are dramatic revelations, hell and the lake of fire are not the focus of Christianity, but we should be aware that hell is a reality and fear Him (God), who can destroy both the body and soul in hell (Mt. 10:28).

Because Jesus became our sin bearer on the cross, all who recognize and accept the Lordship of Jesus are forgiven of their sins and are separated from their sin. Jesus, the Christ, died for us so that we might be reconciled to Father God and dwell together in everlasting life (Jn. 3:16; I Cor. 15:44)... "For the Christian, death, the last enemy, is conquered; Hades is overthrown" (I Cor. 8:40–56; Jn. 11:1–44; Mt. 27:52).[31]

In the worldview of Christianity, history develops in a straight line from creation to redemption to resurrection, to the "great white

---

31 *Life Application Study Bible*, p. 1476; see Vital Statistics. Also, from the International Standard Bible Encyclopedia, in the article "Hades" (pp. 1314-2315) by Gerhartis Vos, we are told that "in the LXX [Septuagint—the oldest Greek version of the Old Testament, completed in the early part of the third century BCE] hades is the standing equivalent for Sheol...the Greek conception of hades was that of a locality receiving into itself all the dead...In Luke 16:23...it has been held that hades is here the comprehensive designation of the locality where the dead reside." In the New Testament, hades becomes associated as the place of punishment in *the abode of the dead*. However, in this book, for the sake of clarity, we will use the word "Gehenna" to designate the place of punishment in the abode of the dead (Sheol, hades).

throne" judgment, to the new heavens and the new earth and beyond. Christianity reveals that there is only one life; no reincarnation, no second chance after death. The person must be "in Christ," meaning that they are justified before God and the righteousness of God has been placed within our being (II Cor. 5:21), and that we have been made a new creation and children of God (II Cor. 5:17) to experience eternal life. Death is the deadline for conversion to Christ, and hopefully it is not a deathbed conversion (though God will accept it) so there is time to labor for Christ in this life.

This chapter will examine the New Testament's revelations about those who do not meet that deadline…those who die "outside" of Christ. They have no redemption, no forgiveness of sins, no hope (Eph. 2:12), no salvation (II Tim. 2:10), no eternal life (I Jn. 5:11).

The writings of Paul will be examined and determinations will be made as to how he achieves the revelation as to what will happen to the wicked (those who are outside of Christ) after their death. In general, Paul's epistles, which date from the early 50s to possibly the late 60s of the first century, are considered the earliest records of Christianity. Regarding the Gospels, Mark was the first Gospel written, probably between AD 55 and 65. The other Gospels quote all but thirty-one verses of Mark.[1] There is no accurate date for the Gospels of Matthew and Luke, but we are confident that they were written after Mark because they show dependence upon Mark by quoting him extensively. Mark's Gospel has some overlap with Paul's writing, where we are not as confident of that with Matthew and Luke. John was written in AD 85–90, after the destruction of the temple in Jerusalem by the Romans but prior to his exile to the island at Patmos. The Gospel of John differs in structure and emphasis from the other three Gospels, which are called the Synoptic Gospels because they give a synopsis of the life of Jesus. The Acts of the Apostles may be contemporary with the Synoptic Gospels (Matthew, Mark, and Luke) with II Peter and Revelation being the most recent books of the New Testament. To follow the chronological development of the revelation about hell (the future location of those outside

Christ), we will first consider the epistles, then the Gospels, and then II Peter and Revelation last.[32]

Paul's Epistles

Paul did not have a clear idea of hell. His concern was more intently focused on the positive side of the Christian message. He never used the word "Gehenna," and in the one place where he refers to "Hades," it is in the context of the defeat of death.[33]

> Death [thanatos] is swallowed up in victory.
> O Death (thanate), where is your victory? O death (hades), where is your sting? (I Cor. 15:54—55, NASB)

The Old Testament authors would use "Sheol" as a synonym for death. Here Paul is using hades as a synonym for death. Paul did not have a systematized theology about hell, yet what he did reveal has divine approval and authority.

1. I Thessalonians

In what is generally accepted as his first epistle (written between AD 50–53), First Thessalonians, Paul does not directly address the subject of hell. However, he does introduce the idea of God's wrath and reaction to resistance to the preaching of truth:

> …and we also thank God continually because, when you received the word of God, which you heard from us, you accepted it not as a human word, but as it actually is, the word of God, which is indeed at work in you who believe. For you, brothers and sisters, became imitators of God's churches in Judea, which are in Christ

---

32 Bernstein, pp. 205-206.
33 Bernstein, p. 207.

> Jesus: You suffered from your own people the same things those churches suffered from the Jews who killed the Lord Jesus and the prophets and also drove us out. They displease God and are hostile to everyone in their effort to keep us from speaking to the Gentiles so that they may be saved. In this way they always heap up their sins to the limit. The wrath of God has come upon them at last. (I Thess. 2:13–16, NASB)

Sadly, it has become more and more popular to criticize, rationalize, censure, and ignore the Bible. In our public schools, the truth of the Bible is not emphasized as a life directive. That alone is detrimental to the nation, as 90 percent of all students attend public schools.[34] The press and entertainment entities ignore or attack the uprightness of the Bible's truths of morality, righteousness, love, and equality of human beings. Parents have set it aside as the guide to child rearing.[35] The truths of the Scripture have been resisted, and according to Paul, that brings the wrath of God. Paul does not delineate clearly the outworking of that wrath.

In addition to direction for life, the Bible is the revelation of God's mercy to sinful persons. That alone would result in God's wrath. Making an effort to halt the revelations of salvation has an eternal consequence for people who are denied the knowledge of salvation in Jesus Christ. This is a dangerous place to be. The Bible addresses many subjects, but redemption is its major theme. It explains God's availability to sinful

---

34 Jack Jennings, "Proportion of U.S. Students in Private Schools Is 10 Percent and Declining," www.huffingtonpost.com/jack-jennings/propertion-of-us, March 18, 2014.
35 Judson Cornwall, *Back to Basics*, Cedric Chivers Limited, Brentwood, Essex, England, 1994, p. 9.

men, that He will forgive and restore lives beaten down by sin.[36] Hence, is it any wonder that His wrath is the result of resisting the truth of His sacrifice? "But it is not clear in this passage [I Thess. 2:16] whether Paul believes these offenders have already experienced divine anger or will do so in The Future." [37]Nor is there a clear statement as to what that wrath may be: suffering before death or eternal punishment after death.

2. I CORINTHIANS

Paul began his ministry in Corinth on his second missionary journey under much opposition (Acts 18:1–18), and he would remain in Corinth for eighteen months.[38] He left Corinth and journeyed to Ephesus. Knowing that Corinth was famous for its intellectual and material prosperity and for its corruption, Paul while in Ephesus found it reliable when he heard of problems and divisions in the church. Having written his first letter to Corinth (referred to in I Cor. 5:9), Paul now writes his second letter (I Corinthians) from Ephesus. He wrote and sent this letter

---

[36] One of the precious promises of the Bible is Joel 2:25: "And I will restore to you the years that the locust has eaten, the cankerworm, and the caterpillar, and the palmerworm, my great Army which I sent among you." I like what David Wilkerson published about this promise. He writes, "I don't care if you have been saved 30 years or 30 days. God can and will restore all your wasted years…You were born for His eternal purposes. He planned for you a life of satisfaction, joy, and usefulness in His Kingdom. But then sin entered, and God's plan for your life was interrupted. The devourer moved in and suddenly your years were wasted, lost. But now, in Christ all is new—even the calendar." See David Wilkerson, "God Will Restore Your Wasted Years!," Missionventureministries.wordpress.com/2011.12/06/god…. With this promise, to realign life and make life successful before God and in the eyes of the people who are watching, is there any wonder that those who are resisting the preaching of truth will face God's wrath?

[37] Bernstein, p. 209, footnote 6.

[38] David K. Lowery, "1 Corinthians," *The Bible Knowledge Commentary*, ed. Walwood and Zuck, NT, ed. (Wheaton: Video Books, 1983), p. 506.

to Corinth about AD 53–54. It appears he learned of these problems from two sources: 1) the household of Chloe (1:11), and a letter sent to him (7:1), possibly by the hands of Stephanas, Fortunatus, and Achaicus (16:17).

While addressing the issues of Corinth, Paul presents a theory of time that is both a mixture of history and prophecy. The future is coupled with the past. With Jesus as the focal point, creation, Jesus's resurrection, and the end of time (I Cor. 15:20–26, 28) are the measuring points in the movement of history thus history has a beginning, middle, and end. The first division of history, from creation to the resurrection, is singled out by the fact that Jesus's resurrection overcomes the death brought about by Adam's sin (I Cor. 15:21–22). Paul makes Jesus's personal resurrection a prefiguring of those who "belong to" Him. In the second division of history, the first event is the resurrection of Jesus; then at the second coming, the resurrection of "those who belong to Christ" will occur. By stipulating that this resurrection will be for "those who are Christ's" (I Cor. 15:23), Paul is implying that not all will be raised. Resurrection to life will be refused to those outside of Christ. In the third and final division of history (the end), Paul prophetically announces that the kingdom, the people of Jesus, are delivered to the Father, and every rule, authority, and power and death have been abolished (I Cor. 15:24–28). Now Father God is "all in all": in other words, He is everything to all of those "in Christ," for those outside of Christ are excluded from being with God.

In view of Paul's interpretation of history, it is possible to address the question of what happens to those who "are not in Christ." In I Corinthians 6:9-11, Paul delineates those who are unrighteous (outside of Christ), who will not inherit the kingdom of God. Therefore we are unambiguously informed that there will be those to whom the Second Coming will not apply, and there is a hint that future destruction awaits, though it is not specifically identified how that destruction will come.

Knowing that exclusion from the kingdom of God awaits all unrighteous souls, it is imperative that we come into the salvation of Jesus

Christ. However, by listing those who are not qualified to inherit the kingdom of God, Paul is warning that we can ignore God's code of righteousness, but the consequences of exclusion will be suffered later on.

> ...Do you not know that the unrighteous will not inherit the Kingdom of God? Do not be deceived; neither fornicators, nor idolaters, adulterers, nor effeminate [effeminate by perversion], nor homosexuals, nor thieves, nor the covetous, nor drunkards, nor revilers, nor swindlers, will inherit the Kingdom of God. (I Cor. 6:9–10, NASB)

The aforementioned list reflects the attitude that God's directives inhibit the fulfillment of life. However, following God's directives for life does not make life miserable. His directives are good maintenance for the life He has given us. And when we follow God's directives (the Ten Commandments, the Sermon on the Mount, etc.), God explains that we will have joy and peace. This doesn't mean that we will not have trouble, but we will experience joy and peace overall.

The person who does not steal does not need to worry about being pursued. The person who tells the truth does not have to recall what they have said to different people. The person who avoids adultery does not have adultery's destructive forces to address in their marriage and life in general. Righteous living is joy and peace, in the Holy Spirit.

3. II Corinthians

After Paul wrote I Corinthians, he visited Corinth. The people's reaction was not what he had hoped for, and the visit was personally painful to Paul and the Christians at Corinth. When he ventured to Ephesus, Paul wrote a severe letter (the third letter to Corinth), which he refers to in II Corinthians 2:14. Some argue that II Corinthians 10–13 is the severe letter, but that is not provable. Titus took the severe letter to Corinth, and he returned to Paul in Ephesus with the report that the people of Corinth had heeded the letter and changed their ways. Paul then writes what is his fourth letter, but it is called II Corinthians. We do not have the first and third letters.

Among Paul's topics of defending himself, refuting false teachings, and encouraging faithfulness, he will in chapter 5 consider Christ's judgment of the righteous and extend a call for Christians know the terror of the Lord to persuade men (this call was gender inclusive— "anthropus" was used). We believers know the fear of the Lord. It is not improbable to suppose that Paul had in mind the judgment of those outside of Christ and was warning his readers to present the Gospel to fellow humans because of impending judgment. The mention of the "coming wrath" was a regular component of Paul's evangelistic preaching (Acts 17:31; I Thess. 1:9–10).

In II Corinthians 5:17, Paul writes that "God was in Christ reconciling the world to Himself but not counting their trespasses against them…" This verse introduces a new theme; it suggests individual initiative must be exercised to answer God's gift of mercy and justification, and those who do not take action to see that their trespasses are not counted against them will be judged. Thus, a reason for exclusion from God's Kingdom is failure to take action to have trespasses and sins not counted against them.

As the revelation continues to expand about what will happen to the wicked after death, it is obvious that our sins separate us from God and cause Him to hide His face from us (Isa. 59:2). Since heaven is viewed as the dwelling place of God, we will not be able to share His home because our sins, our sinful deeds, have separated us from Him. If we fail to take action to have those sinful deeds separated from ourselves, we will be excluded from the kingdom of God after our death. What is that action we must take? We are to respond to the drawing of the Holy Spirit by acknowledging Jesus Christ as our Lord and Savior. At the birth of Jesus, a heavenly host of angels proclaimed, "For unto you is born this day in the city of David a Savior, which is Christ the Lord" (Lk. 2:11). The entire New Testament relentlessly ties the salvation offered by Jesus to God's bountiful and merciful dealings with humankind. Gabriel, God's mighty angel, told Joseph, "And she will bear a son, and you shall call His name Jesus; He will save His people from their sins" (Mt. 1:21, NASB). The very name "Jesus" means "Savior." Salvation from our sins, so they are not held against us, is only found in a personal relationship with the person named Jesus, the son of the living God. He alone:

1) Releases us from our sin
2) Restores us to life
3) Reinstates us to fellowship with God the Father.

Our part in the relationship is to invite Jesus to be our Lord and Savior, then live for Him.

4. THE EPISTLE TO THE GALATIANS

The question of when Galatians was written largely depends on to whom it was written. If the epistle was written to Northern Galatia (which is the older view), to the churches located in north-central Asia Minor, then it was probably written between AD 53–57, from Ephesus or Macedonia. It is held that Paul visited this area on his second missionary journey, though Acts contains no reference to such a visit.

The Southern Galatia theory is that the letter was written to a church in southern Galatia (Antioch, Iconium, Lystia, and Derbe) that Paul founded on his first missionary journey. Some say that it could then have been written between AD 51–53. Whenever it was written, it is the next epistle that we will consider. Paul is writing to remind Christians of their liberty because Judiazers, who taught that Christians had to come under Jewish laws, were challenging them. As he considers this topic, Paul will provide another benchmark for distinguishing those who will inherit the kingdom of God from those who will not. In his epistles, he has given us two criteria thus far:

1) God will assess our deeds here on earth in this life.
2) There must be a positive response to the Holy Spirit, drawing us to salvation in Jesus.

Now here is the third criterion: inheritance depends upon whether we have crucified the flesh in order that we may be led of the Spirit (Gal.

5:16–24). In this passage, Paul identifies the war of the flesh (the unredeemed part of our soul) against our spirit, which wants to obey God. He identifies the works of the flesh that will disqualify us from inheriting the kingdom of God. He likens the discipline required to subdue the works of the flesh to a personal crucifixion, thus allowing one to walk in the spirit. For those who have had the time to demonstrate their relationship to Christ but who do not crucify the flesh, the result is not inheriting the kingdom of God. The walk will not be perfect, but the walk is to occur.

5. ROMANS

Paul wrote the book of Romans from Corinth in CE 57. He wintered in the home of Gaius, just prior to his going to Jerusalem to deliver the alms that had been provided for the poor. His plan was to go to Rome and then onto Spain (Rom. 15:22–29), but his plans were interrupted when he was arrested in Jerusalem. Phoebe, who was a member of the church in Cenchrea near Corinth (Rom. 16:1), most likely carried the letter to Rome.[39]

The theme of the epistle is that the Gospel is the power of God unto salvation where both Greek and Jew are justified by faith and declared righteous by God. In light of that, Paul, in 2:4–11, looks at the time when people will be separated according to their works. Paul makes it clear that the good will receive "glory, honor, peace,

---

39 CEO, S. Michael Hoodman, "Book of Romans," www.gotquestions.org/Book-of-Romans/html.updated.

immortality, and eternal life. [40] Those who do not obey the truth but obey wickedness, they will receive wrath, fury, tribulation, and distress." Yet again Paul gave no revelation as to the fate of the wicked. He could have paired eternal life with eternal death or stated that wrath, fury, tribulation, and distress would be everlasting, but he did not. It is noteworthy of this passage that Paul does not reveal the postmortem punishment that the wicked (those outside of Christ) will receive after death. The same hesitation is seen in Romans 6:20-22 and as has already been noted, in II Corinthians 5:10-14. [41] Notice, however, this hesitancy was because the punishment of the wicked had not been fully revealed to Paul; else he would have warned of the dire punishment prepared for those outside of Christ.

Paul also returns to the divisions of history that he wrote about in I Corinthians 24: the sequence of creation, resurrection, and the end. Writing in Romans 3:23-26, he shows that in Adam all humans fall short of God's goodness, yet through the divine gift of "grace" extended to us when we appeal to Jesus to wash away our sins by His blood, God willingly overlooks our sin. Paul has already told us in II Corinthians 5:14-21, that we are reconciled to God through Jesus, and in Romans 5:8-9, Paul reemphasizes that we are justified by the blood of Jesus and saved from the wrath to come.

---

40 According to the *Full Life Study Bible*, New International Version, Zondervan Corp., Grand Rapids, MI, 2001, p. 1712-1713, footnote on Romans 2:7, the righteous are those who have been justified by faith (1:16-17, 3:24) and persevere in doing what is right according to God's standard (VV.7, 10; Mt. 24:13; Col. 1:23; Heb. 3:14; Rev. 2:10) They value highly the glory that comes from God (1:23, 2:7, 5:2, 8:18), and they seek eternal life (8:33; I Co. 15:51-57); I Pet. 1:4, Rev. 21:1-22:5). Those seeking immortality do so by grace through faith (3:24-25; Eph. 1:4-7; 2:8-10; II Tim. 2:1). The faithful enter into "glory, honor, and immortality" by "persistence in doing good" (Mt. 24:12-13) through the enabling grace given to them by Christ.

41 Bernstein, pp. 217-219.

6. Chapter Conclusions

Paul then has revealed to us that there will be a future wrath that will be faced by the wicked, those outside of Christ. He notes that "wrath and fury...tribulations and distress awaits the wicked" (Rom. 2:4–11), yet he does not reveal how all of this will manifest.

Paul does reveal that there is a very real danger of facing wrath for those:

1) Who oppose the teaching of the truth (I Thess. 2:14–16).
2) Who place themselves outside of Christ by their deeds (I Cor. 6:9–11; Gal. 5:19–21).
3) Who fail to take the initiative to respond to the drawing of the Holy Spirit to Jesus for the forgiveness of our sins (Rom. 1:16–17, 3:23–26).

Chapter Four

The Synoptics Plus John

Chapter Introduction

For three chapters, we have been building to this point where we will see with clarity the postmortem future of the wicked (those outside of Christ). The New Testament Synoptic Gospel authors (Matthew, Mark, and Luke) reveal that there will be eternal punishment in the flames of fire for those who are outside of Christ's salvation.

Some passages explicitly refer to the place of burning as Gehenna. They describe it as fire, call it eternal, and declare it to be the fate of those found wanting at the last judgment. Three crucial passages in the Synoptic Gospels helped form the concept [the revelation] of hell: Mark 9:43–48 and Matthew 25:31–46 call the place of punishment Gehenna, Luke 16:19–31 refers to hades but the suffering of the sinner described there put this passage at the punitive extreme…of the Hebrew Sheol. [42]

Luke 16, in actuality, reveals that the punishment is eternal. [43]

In this chapter, we will review the revelation of hell as seen in the Synoptic Gospels without great comment. The revelation seen in the

---

42 Bernstein, p. 228.

43 Luke records Jesus' story of the rich man and Lazarus. He quotes Jesus repeating Abraham's words to the deceased rich man in the blaze of hades: "…between us and you there is a great chasm fixed, in order that…none may cross over from there to us" (Lk. 16:26).

Synoptic Gospels about hell will erase the **false teaching of universalism**. That is the wrong teaching that asserts everyone will be saved from a fiery judgment because God is too loving to exclude anyone from heaven. The other teachings will also be proved false by the revelation of the Synoptic Gospels.

Restorationism, the teaching that punishment in hell is not eternal will be proved wrong by the Synoptic Gospel revelations about this horrible place of punishment. Thirdly, the Synoptic Gospels' revelation of hell will eradicate confidence in **probationism**. That is the false teaching that proclaims all those who died outside of Christ will have a second chance to accept the salvation offered by Jesus. Lastly, the fourth false teaching that the Synoptic refutes is **annihilationism**. This false teaching seeks to take the fear of hell out of the hearts of people by arguing that the final punishment of human beings results in their total destruction (annihilation) rather than everlasting agony. Annihilationism asserts that God will eventually destroy or annihilate the wicked, leaving the righteous to live alone in immortality.[44] Annihilation looks to passages like II Thessalonians 1:9: "and these will pay the penalty of eternal destruction, away from the presence of the Lord and from the glory of His power" (NASB). The scriptural usage of the word "destruction" does not mean annihilation, but ruin. [45]

Although all four of these false doctrines are shown by the Synoptic Gospels' revelation of hell to be spurious, they will still be taught as a part of a devilish plan to take souls from dwelling forever with Father God. Satan delights in that, but God, who has voluntarily tied Himself to individuals' free will as to whether they accept His salvation (Deut. 30:19; Joshua 24:15; Prov. 3:31; James 4:17), does not want any to perish but He wants all to come to repentance (II Peter 3:9). The four teachings just cited are false teachings, and the Synoptic revelations will demonstrate that.

---

44 Carolina Wrend, "Annihilationism," en.wikipedia.org/wiki/annihilationism.

45 Judson Cornwall, *Back to Basics*, pp. 311-312.

The Gospel According to Mark

"John Mark is mentioned ten times in the New Testament—in Acts as a young man in whose house the church in Jerusalem met (Acts 12:12) and who accompanied Paul and Barnabas on their first missionary journey (Acts 12:25, 13:5, 13; 15:37-39) [and] in Colossians and Philemon Mark is mentioned as someone with Paul during his first Roman imprisonment (Col. 4:10; Phm. 24) and in Second Timothy as someone Paul desired to have with him during his second Roman imprisonment (II Tim. 4:11). Also, First Peter indicates that Mark is someone beloved by Peter, and with him in Rome (I Pet. 5:13),[46] wrote the Gospel according to Mark probably around 60 AD.[47] This means that it is appropriate to have considered Paul's epistles first, since he began to write before Mark composed his Gospel.

After the transfiguration (Mk. 9:2-9), and passing through Galilee (Mk. 9:30), Jesus arrives in His adult hometown of Capernaum and enters a house He apparently frequented while in Capernaum (John Gill

---

46 Ted Cabal, *The Apologetics Study Bible*, Holman Bible Publishers, Nashville, TN, 2007, pp. 1463-1464. *The Apologetics Study Bible* further says that Papias, the bishop of Hierapolis, in Asia Minor writing around AD 130 mentions Mark is the author, and this is the earliest mention of Mark being the author. Eusebius, the early church historian, quoted Papias, noting that Mark, as a follower of Peter, recorded stories about Jesus that Peter used in his preaching. (See p. 1463.)

47 Ted Cabal, p. 1464. There are various considerations for dating Mark's Gospel. Irenaus, Bishop of Lyon, France (ca. AD 180), says Mark was written after the departure of Peter and Paul from Rome. It is uncertain as to whether Irenaus meant after they left Rome to go to another location or after they died. In either case it places the time of authorship in the early 60s (p. 1464). The early AD 60s date would also correspond with the estimated date that Matthew wrote his Gospel (AD 60s is not unreasonable) and when Luke wrote his Gospel (prior to AD 62) (pp. 1403, 1508). Both Matthew and Luke use Mark's Gospel in their own Gospels. There are some who back Mark's date of composition into the AD 50s to better accommodate Mark's usage by Matthew and Luke.

hypothesizes that it was the house of Simon and Andrew; John Gill's Exposition of the Bible, www.biblestudytools.com/.../Mark-9-33.html) and there, Jesus reiterates the dangers of sin to His disciples (see Mark 9:43–48). "This passage in Mark, considered to be the earliest Gospel, was the first to identify the fire and the worm of Isaiah 66:24 with Gehenna ["Gehenna" in Mark 9:43 is translated "hell"] …there can be no question about the threat of hellfire here." [48] Isaiah 66:24 also enunciates that the fire is endless and the worms never die. The Holy Spirit has inspired Jesus to connect Isaiah 66:24, and the Holy Spirit has inspired Mark to write down Jesus's words with specificity. Therefore, this is the earliest New Testament reference to an everlasting hell. Matthew also used this passage (Mt. 5:29–30) in his Gospel (written after Mark). Unlike Paul, Mark lists the horrible postmortem consequences of people who die outside of Christ.

The Bible consistently teaches that an insufferable doom is the consequence of a sinner dying without Jesus being his or her Savior.

"The most graphic descriptions of the torments the lost will suffer came from the lips of the loving Savior Himself. He knew too much to be mistaken. He was too righteous to deceive us, and He was too kindhearted to conceal the truth and not to warn us of the impending doom that the lost will face." [49]

Jesus was not dependent upon the definition of Hebrew words when He wanted to declare divine revelation. He did not hide behind the ambiguity of vocabulary, but He taught with divine authority, frequently illustrating His revelation with a parable designed to clarify the matter. So when He contrasted the unspeakable torment of hell with the valley of Hinnom, he did it to define in a word picture what a horrible future those who are outside of His salvation will eternally suffer.

The suffering of eternal hell is so severe that Mark and Matthew repeat, under the inspiration of the Holy Spirit, that it would be better

---

48 Bernstein, pp. 218-219. "Gehenna" is the Greek rendering of *Ge-Hinnom*.
49 Judson Cornwall, *Back to Basics*, p. 315.

for a person to lose an eye, hand, or foot (which they are using as instruments of sin) than to be cast into eternal punishment.

THE GOSPEL ACCORDING TO MATTHEW

Irenaeus (ca. CE 125–202), referred to as Saint Irenaus by some, was the Bishop of Lugdunum in Gaul, then a part of the Roman Empire (now Lyon, France). He reported that Matthew was written while Peter and Paul preached at Rome, placing the Gospel's creation in the CE 60s. This is not unreasonable,[50] but it was written after the Gospel according to Mark was composed.

After presenting the genealogy of Jesus through Joseph and the birth narrative, the Holy Spirit has Matthew announce through the preaching of John the Baptist the eternal fiery postmortem fate of those who do not look for the coming Messiah. Even before the teaching of Jesus is presented, the Holy Spirit alerts us through John's preaching to the Pharisees and Sadducees that Jesus will come and separate the wheat (the righteous) from the chaff (the unrighteous/wicked/outside of Christ).

"And His winnowing fork is in His hand, and He will thoroughly clear His threshing floor and He will gather His wheat into the barn, but He will burn up the chaff with unquenchable fire" (Mt. 3:12, NASB).

John the Baptist is the forerunner (Isa. 1–5; Mt. 4:5–6) for Jesus. It was John's responsibility to call out of Israel a believing remnant who would be spiritually prepared for the Messiah's coming. The heart of the person was prepared through repentance and faith, and that preparation was manifested by water baptism. Many responded, but the Jewish officials did not respond. To wit, John the Baptist announces that those who refuse to spiritually prepare for and then surrender to the Messiah will face a fiery judgment analogous to chaff burning (Mt. 2:1–12).

At Jesus's baptism He is clearly presented to be the Messiah:

---

50 Ted Cabal, *The Apologetics Study Bible*, pp. 1402-1403.

...After being baptized Jesus went up immediately from the water and behold the heavens were opened, and He saw the Spirit of God descending as a dove, and coming upon Him, and behold a voice out of the heavens saying, "this is my beloved Son in whom I am well pleased." (Mt. 3:16–17, NASB)

Since the law of Moses taught that two or three witnesses confirm a matter beyond further question, Jesus now had the ultimate confirmation; He had the testimony of John the Baptist, the testimony of the Spirit who rested upon Him, and the testimony of the Father's speaking from heaven. It was final. Jesus's divine identification has been established. To reject Jesus as Messiah and Savior is to face a future of retribution whose metaphor is chaff that is ablaze. Matthew is clear; we are not to be indifferent toward Jesus. The Messiah is to become our Lord, or else a fiery postmortem future awaits.

Matthew also provides for us what may be the single most important biblical passage for the revelation of hell. On Tuesday of the Passion Week (the time from Palm Sunday through Easter Sunday), Jesus gave the Olivet Discourse (Matthew 24:1–25:46) which is the fifth and last of the discourses in Matthew's Gospel (5–7, 10; 13; 18; 24–25). Parallel passages of the Olivet Discourse are found in Mark 13:1–37 and Luke 21:5–36. However, the record in Matthew is the most extensive.

Matthew reports on the reply of Jesus, on the Mount of Olives, to the disciples, about His return. Jesus tells the disciples about the perilous times that are coming. He relates the parable of the fig tree and tells them that all believers are to be on the alert and ready for His return. Then, in Matthew 25, Jesus illustrates the importance of being ready by telling the parable of the ten virgins, and then he tells the parable of the talents, where the servants who do not prepare for the return of their master (the Messiah) will be banished to outer darkness, and in that place there will be weeping and gnashing of teeth. Earlier, in Matthew 13:42, the imagery of "weeping and gnashing of teeth" (Jesus is explaining the parable of the weeds, Matthew 13:24, 30, 36–43), occurs in the context of a fiery furnace. [51] Jesus is giving us yet another insight into the situation of those who suffer postmortem punishment because of a failure to surrender to Him as Savior and Lord: weeping and gnashing of teeth in a fiery furnace. Hell is a place of torment and agony.

In looking over Matthew's recordings of what Jesus said about the place of punishment for the wicked, we return to the Sermon on the Mount and look at Matthew 7:19-20. In that passage, in the interpretive glow of Matthew 13:42, we see that Jesus was referring to hell when He said that "every tree that does not bear good fruit is cut down and thrown into the fire. So then you will know them by their fruits." How desperate it is for we believers to produce good fruit. Our good fruit, done in Jesus's name, will identify us before men as being "in Christ."

However, more than good works are demanded of the believer; there must be a surrender to Jesus—heart, soul, mind, and strength. Just three verses later in the Sermon on the Mount, Jesus says to those who professed to know Him but did not, "I never knew you; depart from me..." (Matthew 9:23). Another part of the punishment upon these outside of Christ is to be separated from the presence of Jesus.

Returning to our consideration of the Olivet Discourse in Matthew 24 and 25, after Jesus has made the points that:
1) The believer should be watching (24:37–44)
2) The believer should be faithful, doing the Master's will (24:45–51)
3) The believer should be prepared (25:1–13)
4) The believer should be discharging his or her responsibilities (25:14–30)

he tells the parable of the sheep and goats (Mt. 25:31–46). It is the account of judgment itself where Jesus will say to those whom He

---

51 The phrase "weeping and gnashing of teeth" occurs six times in Matthew's Gospel: 13:42, 50; 8:12; 22:13; 24:51, 25:30) and nowhere else in the New Testament. See Kenneth L. Barker, *Zondervan NIV Study Bible*, Zondervan, Grand Rapids, MI, 2002, p. 1491, footnote 13:42.

condemns, "Depart from me, accursed ones, into eternal fire which has been prepared for the devil and his angels" (Mt. 25:41, NASB).

Then Jesus explains why they were damned—they omitted charity. "Those failing in charity...could see no potential benefit in aiding the hungry, thirsty, and needy and so did not sacrifice...for those with whom Christ identified Himself."[52]

To end the parable, Jesus editorializes about the goats and sheep: "And these will go away into eternal punishment, but the righteous into eternal life" (Mt. 25:46).

> This teaching of Jesus on the sheep and the goats appears only in Matthew. He was not teaching salvation by works in these verses. The compassion shown by the sheep shows their salvation. That both the sheep and the goats are surprised at their "qualifications" indicate that neither was working for salvation. Those who were punished for their failure to minister to others were so blinded by their preoccupation with themselves that they showed no compassion. The

---

52 Bernstein, p. 233.

parable shows that mere profession of one's belief that does not lead to love and concern for people is useless.[53]

In reality Jesus is emphasizing the truth of practical, God-approved Christianity that emanates from a heart surrendered to Him. As others have noticed, and the longer I live, and after having pastored for thirty-one years, the stronger becomes my conviction that few want a practical religion; many want a self-serving, supernatural religion. In America, Christianity is embraced as a philosophy, but it is all too often rejected as a way of life. We are happy to build churches, publish Bibles, and hire pastors, but many do not want to live by the code that Jesus taught. [54]

---

53 Ted Cabal, *The Apologetics Study Bible*, pp. 1449-1450, footnote 25:31–46. See also *The Life Application Bible*, Tyndale House Publishers Inc. and Zondervan Publishing House, Wheaton, IL and Grand Rapids, MI, p. 1708, footnote 25:46. As a clarification of terms since Jesus is being so revelatory of the situation in hell, "eternal punishment takes place in hell (the lake of fire, or Gehenna), the place of punishment after death for all those who refuse to repent. In the Bible three words are used in connection with eternal punishment: 1) Sheol, or 'the grave' is used in the Old Testament to mean the place of the dead, generally thought to be under the earth (see Job 24:19, Ps. 16:10; Isaiah 38:10); 2) Hades is the Greek word for underworld, the realm of the dead. It is the word used in the New Testament for Sheol (see Matthew 16:18; Revelation 1:18; 20; 13, 14); 3) Gehenna, or hell, was named after the Valley of Hinnom near Jerusalem where children were sacrificed by fire to the pagan gods (see II Kings 23:10; II Chron. 28:3). This is the place of eternal fire (Mt. 5:22, 10:28; Mk. 9:43: Lk. 12:5, Jas. 3:6; Rev. 19:20) prepared for the devil and his angels and all those who do not believe in God (35:46; Rev. 20:9, 10). This is the final and eternal state of the wicked after the resurrection and the last Judgment. When Jesus warns us against unbelief he is trying to save us from agonizing punishment." As a caveat to the Life Application Bible footnote just quoted, hell is not the final place for the wicked, those outside of Christ. After the final judgment, hell will be cast into the lake of fire, and that is the eternal place of the wicked. See Rev. 20:14.

54 Judson Cornwall, *The Best of Judson Cornwall*, Bridge Publishing Inc., South Plainfield, NJ, 1992, pp. 31-32.

This parable of the sheep and the goats brings home the stark reality that Jesus demands—and will hold each believer eternally accountable for—the practical care of one's neighbor to accompany a profession of Jesus being our Lord. How many times have pastors experienced church leaders who attend board meetings and read the financial sheets, but those same leaders resist visiting a prison or hospital or an individual's home, or an eldercare facility, or refuse to participate in meeting the practical food and life needs of fellow human beings beyond directing minimal church funds, or resist the transfer of resources to a missionary trying to meet the Matthew 25 imperatives? Yet those same leaders, like the Pharisees of the New Testament, enjoy sitting in the place of spiritual leadership, but their care for people is abysmal. This parable teaches all believers that we had better serve the interest of fellow human beings out of a surrendered heart to Jesus, or an eternal punishment is a real possibility.

The Gospel According to Luke

Writing after Mark, but uncertain as to whether he wrote before or after Matthew, conservative scholarship asserts that Luke composed his Gospel around or before CE 62. [55] He wrote to present an authoritative account of the life and ministry of Jesus Christ. As to whether or not Luke directed his book to a person named Theophilus or to the general believing community (the name Theophilus means "loved by God," thus using the name symbolically), there is no final answer. He wrote about Jesus being our Lord and Savior and cited history to connect Jesus

---

55 The date of Luke is debated among scholars. The latest possible date for Luke is about AD 80 since there is evidence of its existence from 95 on. On the other hand, the book probably was not written earlier than the late 50s, since Luke was apparently written not long before Acts (Acts 1:1), and 62 is the date of the last event recorded in Acts (Paul's house arrest in Rome). Thus a date of 62 or earlier is generally accepted. See *The Apologetics Study Bible*, p. 1508; *Life Application Study Bible*, p. 1782; Robert Gromack, *New Testament Survey*, Baker Beck House, Grand Rapids, MI, 1974, p. 111.

to places and events. He details Jesus's love and compassion for people and emphasizes the presence of the Holy Spirit. Luke also records Jesus presenting one of the three crucial passages in the New Testament that helps to form the revelation about hell, the story of the rich man and Lazarus (Lk. 16:19-33).[56]

In the telling of the story, Luke calls the area "Hades": "The term was known throughout the Greek world and used by Greek-speaking Jews to translate the Hebrew Sheol…[but] his idea of hades is conceptually closer to Gehenna of…Mark, or Matthew, than to the Sheol of the Hebrew Bible or even Paul's one reference to Hades, where it is equated with death in general." [57] Although hades is not a neutral place in Luke's thought, and is the realm of punishment for the wicked dead, it was still the most efficient communicative to speak of hell in the Greek mind, but Gehenna is still the term for the fiery punishment of the wicked dead.

While on his journey to Jerusalem to die on the cross, Jesus tells the story of the rich man and Lazarus. (See Lk. 16:19-33.) And, in this story, Jesus clearly adds to our understanding of hell. [58]

In the relating of the event, Jesus refers to the agony of Dives (the rich man). In his desperation, seeing Abraham and Lazarus, Dives asks for Abraham to send Lazarus to him with a drop of water to cool his

---

56 Previously cited in the text but for a reminder, the three crucial passages are Mark 9:43-48, Matthew 25:31-46, and Luke 16:19-31.

57 Bernstein, pp. 239, 245.

58 The Latin term for "rich man" is "Dives." The rich man, though unnamed in Scripture, is often called Dives in various theatrical and literary works. There is also controversy as to whether Jesus' story is a parable or actual story. Because Lazarus (name means "God Helps") is mentioned and the rich man is not named but is instead referred to as "a certain right man," there is a body of opinion that says it was a real event because Jesus is protecting the identity rich man (he would have been known). Lazarus was not known, so Jesus could use his name. This is accepted by many and the author of this book as being a real event. Those who regard it as a real event also hold that it is a recent event for Jesus. It is before the resurrection, the second coming, and the last judgment.

burning tongue, and he also asks that Lazarus be sent to warn his five brothers about "this place of torment" (Lk. 16:28, NASB). Abraham denies both requests, and in those denials we gain further insight into hell and what will happen to the wicked in hell.

The refusal of a drop of water lies in two realms. First there is a great chasm, an impermeable barrier between the two locations; Dives can neither receive help nor escape from hell. Help is not available for Dives. Dante is euphemistically correct in his sentiment when he hypothesizes in his poem "The Inferno" that there is a sign over the entrance of hell that says "Abandon all hope." The great chasm removes all hope for help or rescue. The second realm of reasoning as to why there will be no water is because a neglected and ignored responsibility to alleviate the suffering of the poor, the underprivileged, those neglected by society, and those who have fallen into the cracks. The refusal to help the unfortunate on the earth implies just deprivation in death.

In Amos, we see that he (and other prophets will also) identifies the mistreatment of the underprivileged and defenseless with wickedness (Amos 5:12). Ezekiel, when explaining the reason for God's anger with Israel, includes the charge of oppressing the poor and needy (Ezk. 22:29). In the book of Proverbs, Solomon warns that to take advantage and oppress the poor will be met with divine judgment. (See Proverbs 21:13, 22:16, 22–23.) Though none of those scriptural citations imply postmortem punishment, we see from Abraham's statement to Dives that such violations will also be addressed by eternal punishment.

The denial of the second request of Dives, which was to send Lazarus to warn his five living brothers, also occurs in two realms. First, Lazarus is dead; there is no ability for the dead to return to the living, and this shows that death is the deadline for establishing a salvation relationship with Jesus. Dives knows that he too has finished his life on earth, and thus is beyond the salvation deadline. He has no hope, but it is not too late for his five brothers because they are still alive on the earth.

The second realm of the denial for the request that Lazarus return to warn Dives's five living brothers entails a contempt for the Scripture. Dives has to be instructed that Scripture is more influential than the dead returning to issue a warning. The five brothers have Scripture, and that is more than enough warning for them. It is a clear statement about the priority and importance of the Scriptures. Jesus is teaching that earthly life is fleeting and that death is the deadline for any decision to accept salvation through Jesus's blood and implement works of righteousness (if there is time) and the knowledge of that comes from the Scriptures. [59]

The Bible (Scriptures, the Word of God) is a unique book, and because it deals with our eternal salvation, it should be given priority over every other book (regardless of credible translation or the delivery system to listen to the Bible). The Apostle Peter writes, "For no prophecy was ever made by an act of human will, but men moved by the Holy Spirit spoke from God" (II Peter 1:21, NASB). God moved through persons of His choosing to make known the subjects we need to know to be a child of God and act as a child of God. We should perceive the future and heed the repeated warnings to avoid the place of torment. It is essential for people to know and believe the Scriptures. Scripture resonates with the soul, providing conviction for salvation. To ignore the truth of the Scripture (if it is available) is to guarantee an agonizing, eternal postmortem existence in hell.

THE GOSPEL ACCORDING TO JOHN

The fourth of the four Gospels, John (written in ca. CE 90) is different from the Synoptic Gospels (Matthew, Mark, and Luke). The Synoptics give a synopsis of the life of Jesus, sharing much of the same content (see "Synoptic Gospels," wikipedia.org/wiki/synoptic-Gospels). The Holy Spirit inspired John to pursue differences in his Gospel. John does not mention the Virgin Birth, Jesus's baptism, Jesus's temptation in the wilderness, the parables, the transfiguration, and the institution of Holy Communion. He includes content not found in the Synoptics, such as the wedding in Cana, the encounter with Nicodemus and the

---

59 Bernstein, pp. 239-241.

Samaritan woman, the resurrection of Lazarus, the healing of the paralytic at the pool, the healing of the blind man, Jesus's farewell discourse, and parts of the pastoral narrative. [60]

The fourth Gospel is unique. It contains a variety of statements and information about Jesus not contained in the Synoptic Gospels. John's Gospel presents a different side of Jesus that is complementary to the other three Gospels and provides a clearer understanding of His divinity and preexistence. The Holy Spirit is moving upon John to write a gospel that doesn't just tell the life and ministry of Jesus, but leads readers to understand that Jesus is the source of salvation and that He is the Messiah (Jn. 20:30–31).[61]

John is also different from the Synoptic Gospels in that he, like Paul (Paul died about twenty-five to thirty years prior), does not actually describe the wrath of God, and the one reference he makes to burning (Jn. 15:1–6) needs the clarification provided in the Synoptics.

John emphasizes that belief and acting upon that belief in Jesus as savior is the key to eternal life (Jn. 5:24). In fact, John highlights that we are to love the light (3:19), hear the word (5:24), and live virtuously (5:29). John's revelation is very clear: for those who believe there will be eternal life, but for those who do not believe, there will be judgment, wrath, and death.

John, different from the Synoptics, expresses the wrath of God as a denial of eternal life, but like Paul (whom Rome had executed approximately three decades earlier), John makes no reference to what the content of that denial of eternal life will be except for his telling of Jesus's personal metaphor in John 15:1–6:

---

60 Bethany Seeley, "Why Is John's Gospel Different from the Synoptic Gospels," www.ehow.com/info.8475770.johns.gospel-different…

61 "Gospel of John," Theopedia, www.theopedia.com/Gospel.of.jon. Theopedia describes itself as a "growing online evangelical encyclopedia of Biblical Christianity." See "about" at Theopedia.com for further information.

> If anyone does not abide in Me, he is thrown away as a branch and dries up: and they gather them and cast them into the fire, and they are burned. (Jn. 15:6, NASB)

That is John's strongest reference to the postmortem punishment of the wicked. Because we have the Synoptics, we are clear what John means but, had we not had the Synoptics, Jesus's metaphor would not have been clear. John, like Paul, understood there would be judgment and wrath, but the shape and contours of that wrath were not addressed as they were in the Synoptics.[62]

John leaves no doubt as to where salvation is to be found. Jesus is the Savior and redeemer, and only through Jesus can anyone be "born again." Jesus told Nicodemus that he had to be "born again" to see the Kingdom of God (Jn. 3:3, 5), and Jesus told Nicodemus how to be born again by saying "that which is born of the flesh is flesh; and that which is born of the spirit is spirit" (Jn. 3:6, NASB). The new birth is exclusively the work of the Holy Spirit. We personally accept the conviction of the Holy Spirit that Jesus died to pay our penalty for sin, but He rose and ascended back to heaven, all to bring us a life that is new as the birth of an infant into this world. Codified religion plays no part in this great miracle. There is nothing further to be done; we gain salvation by grace (not grace plus works). On the cross, Jesus announced, "It is finished" (Jn. 19:30).[63]

CHAPTER CONCLUSION

The Synoptic Gospels clarify with stark truth the content of the postmortem wrath of God that is the future of those who die outside of Christ. The Synoptic Gospels make it clear that those who do not surrender to Jesus as Lord and Savior in this life will have no opportunity

---

62 Bernstein, pp. 224-227.

63 Judson Cornwall, *Back to Basics*, pp. 28-29.

for a second chance at salvation after death. Death is the line of demarcation for salvation.

John, on the other hand, makes a direct reference that the branch unattached to Jesus (a person not in the family of God, even though he or she may be religious) will be thrown away and cast into the fire where he or she will be burned. John recognizes there will be wrath and burning in the postmortem future of the wicked dead, but he is not as clear about that future as the Synoptic Gospels.

Chapter Five

Jesus's Descent into Hell, the Lake of Fire

Chapter Introduction

The biblical view of world history includes creation, the fall of angels, expulsion from Eden, the virgin birth, the cross and resurrection, the birth of the church, the rapture (which includes the resurrection of the righteous), the second coming, the millennial reign, the great white throne judgment (where those outside of Christ are raised to face their eternal judgment), then the new heavens and the new earth. [64] This biblical world history lies in the background as God's revelation unfolds,

---

64 Paul and the New Testament authors would explain key moments in the biblical history of the world. Paul overviews the chronology of biblical world history from Adam, through Christ, to the end of time in Romans 5:17–19, 11:32 and II Corinthians 15:22 26, 45. Critical moments in biblical world history are referred to by other New Testament authors: John 17:24 refers to what happened "before the foundation of the world," Matthew 25:41 refers to "the external fire prepared for the Devil and his angels," and in Matthew 25:4, he alluded to the righteous, saying "the Kingdom prepared for you from the foundation of the world."

showing us that though the divine plan may seem to be "off the rails," in reality, the plan of God moves forward as God has ordained.[65]

The study of what will happen to the wicked (those outside of Christ) now turns to what is yet to come, explained to us by the latter books of the New Testament, where the prophesied future stands on that which is in the background.

PETER'S EPISTLES

Shortly after his first epistle and shortly before his martyrdom, Peter wrote his second epistle (II Peter). It was probably written somewhere in the range of CE 64–67, possibly in Rome, but that is speculation. In the letter, Peter acknowledges that this is his second epistle (3:1), and he makes several references to his past personal relationship to Christ. He speaks of being an eyewitness to the transfiguration (II Pet. 1:15–18; Mt. 17:1-3), and he knows that his martyrdom is imminent because of Jesus's prediction (1:13–14; Jn. 21:18-19). Peter wrote this epistle, as is attested to by third-century church fathers and Jerome, Athanasius, Augustine, and Ambrose in the fourth century.[66]

Peter, in the letter, shows that he is aware that he and other apostles have been accused of telling stories that "a clever person made" (1:16); Peter retorts that it was the false teachers that made up stories (2:3) and that their destruction slumbers not. Their heresy involved a denial of

---

65 Just as God has established the direction of world history and it is in the background of all that happens on the earth, there's another example of an event that is background to spiritual warfare. Alan Bernstein points out that in Luke 10:1-11, Jesus instructed the seventy disciples to go from town to town, preaching and healing. Then, in Luke 10:17, the seventy returned "with joy," telling Jesus that even demons were subject to them in His name. The explanation Jesus gives cites a long-past event where Satan had been reduced: "I was watching Satan fall from heaven like lightning" (Lk. 10:18, NASB). Satan had been defeated long before, so his kingdom has to yield to Jesus…that is always in the background (Bernstein, pp. 259-261).

66 Robert G. Gromacki, *New Testament Survey*, pp. 359-361.

Christ, probably the deity of His person, the nature of His atonement (2:1), and the reality of His second coming (3:4). To that, Peter assures the church that, just as the Lord preserved righteous Noah with seven others and just as God preserved Lot from Sodom and Gomorrah's destruction, so the Lord knows how to preserve His followers (who Peter is writing to is not identified in the text) and keep the unrighteous (the false teachers) under punishment for the day of judgment (2:1–10). Here the background information is in view, for in II Peter 2:4, Peter reminds God's people that He (God) did not spare angels when they sinned but cast them into hell to be held until the day of judgment. So the church can rest confident that God can deal with these false prophets who would lure His people from Himself. "Cast them into hell" translates a Greek coinage "Tartarosas" (from *tartaroo*), which is used only this once in the New Testament, a verb built on the noun Tartarus. The rebellious angels have been "Tartared" or "Tartarized" or "Entartered." [67] Aware that some of the angels who sinned are in Tartarus awaiting the final judgment, Peter can assure God's people that He will also hold false teachers accountable at the last judgment. Satan will not be the victor.

The satanic kingdom has been completely defeated and reduced. That is demonstrated by an event that Peter records in his first epistle (I Pet. 3:18, 19), written around CE 64. Peter records that while in the state of physical death, as Jesus's body was lying in the tomb, Jesus descended

---

[67] Bernstein, p. 251. See also "Pulpit Commentary Reference," biblehub.com/2Peter/2-4.htm. Saint Peter is giving proofs of his assertion that the punishment of the ungodly lingereth not. The first is the punishment of angels that sinned. He does not specify the sin, whether rebellion as in Revelation 12:7, or uncleanliness, as apparently was the case in Jude 1:6, 7 and Genesis 6:4…The Greek word that is found nowhere else in the Greek Scriptures…[and belongs] to heathen mythology is…without parallel in the New Testament…apparently Saint Peter regards Tartarus not as equivalent to Gehenna, for the sinful angels are reserved unto judgment, but as a place of preliminary detention.

in spirit to Tartarus (the place where the fallen angels are imprisoned).[68] Tartarus is not hell, but it is a "cellblock" or a "compartment" (II Peter 2:4; Jude 6) of hell. It is a place:

a. Of imprisonment, where fallen angels are chained (II Pet. 2, Jude 6)
b. Of darkness (II Peter 2:4; Jude 6)
c. Of vengeance (Jude 7)
d. Of eternal fire (Jude 7) [69]

To whom did Jesus preach when He descended? Four separate areas are in view, though it may well be that Tartarus, the Pit, and Gehenna are each a single location in one compartment of Sheol. The second compartment of Sheol is believed to have been paradise.

Jesus went to **Tartarus** and preached to the fallen angels who had rebelled against God from the eons past in eternal history (Isa. 14:4–17; Ezekiel 28:14; Revelation 12:7–13) and are now imprisoned. He preached His victory and their defeat.

If the angels of Tartarus are the "sons of God" mentioned in Genesis 6:1–4, then they were trying to destroy the human race and prevent the promised seed, the Savior, from coming. Jesus would then preach His victory by proclaiming before them that their plan did not work (II Pet. 2:4; Jude 6–7).

He probably proclaimed His triumph to all the unbelievers in **Gehenna**. He vindicated the way of faith, proclaiming that the faith of Noah and all the other believers was victorious. Remember that Noah's faith and life was never vindicated in his lifetime. He was mocked and abused by the people of his day. Therefore, Jesus Himself (may well have) personally proclaimed the victory.

In the **abyss, or the bottomless pit** (Lk. 8:33; Rev. 9:1–3, 11; 11:7, 17:8; 20:1–12), the abode of the demons, Jesus vindicated the faith of all

---

[68] Dr. Grant C. Richardson, Verse by Verse Commentary (I Peter 3:19), versebyversecomentary.com/1-peter/1-peter-319; Finis Jennings Dake, *Dake's Annotated Reference Bible*, Dake Bible Sales Inc., Lawrenceville, GA, Mar. 2004, p. 267, Note K.

[69] *The Preacher's Outline and Sermon Bible*, Leadership Ministries Worldwide, Chattanooga, TN, vol. III, p. 747.

believers who have been oppressed by the evil spirits down through the millennia.

In **paradise**, a separate compartment of Sheol (the place of the dead), there Jesus probably showed Himself to the Old Testament saints in paradise, proclaiming the fullness of their salvation. Then He transferred paradise in Sheol to heaven (some think that heaven's paradise is the Garden of God located outside the fifteen-hundred-mile-high walls). So the Old Testament believers are now located in heaven, with the New Testament believers (Ps. 30:3; Eph. 4:8).[70]

Peter has clearly achieved the revelation of what will happen to the wicked. He is confident that God will deal with false teachers, just as He dealt with the sins of Sodom and Gomorrah. He also gives assurance that the kingdom of Satan has been totally defeated by relating the event of Jesus descending into hell and preaching His victory to all the inhabitants of Sheol, regardless of which compartment they were located in.

THE REVELATION TO JOHN ABOUT THE LAKE OF FIRE

Around CE 95–96, while on the Isle of Patmos, the Apostle John (author identified himself four times, Rev. 1:1, 4, 9; 22:8) received the revelation of the end of the age, things that would shortly come to pass. In the revelation that Jesus gave to John, we gain further insight of what will happen to the wicked (those outside of Christ).

Early in the book, after identifying Himself, John records Jesus'ss letter to the second of the seven churches of Asia, where the "second death" is introduced. Only four times in the Bible is the term "second death" employed (Rev. 2:11; Rev. 20:6, 14; Rev. 21:8). Physical death on this earth where the soul and spirit are separated from the body is the

---

70 *The Preacher's Outline and Sermon Bible*, vol. 3, p. 749. In Ephesians 4:8–10, Paul reasons that His ascent makes a precious descent, and that this refers to Christ who first descended, then ascended. This verse also means more than just descended to the earth, it refers to the regions beneath it.

first death, and it is temporary because there will ultimately be a resurrection from that death...either to eternal life, or if one is outside of Christ, and therefore wicked, resurrected to eternal death. However, the second death, as explained in Revelation 21:8, means that the person is cast into the fiery lake of burning sulfur. Those who are "inside Christ" are not affected by the second death. And the term certainly contrasts the distress of the eternal fate of those outside of Christ compared to the happiness of those inside of Christ.

John, writing of the great white throne judgment, which occurs after the millennial reign, explains that the lake of fire, into which death, hell, and all those whose names are not found in The Lamb's Book of Life, will be eternally cast, defines the lake of fire as the second death:

> Then I saw a great white throne and Him who sat upon it, from whose presence earth and heaven fled away, and no place was found for them. And I saw the dead, the great and the small, standing before the throne, and books were opened; and another book was opened, which is the book of life; and the dead were judged from the things which were written in the books, according to their deeds. And the sea gave up the dead which were in it, and death and Hades gave up the dead which were in them; and they were judged, every one of them according to their deeds. Then death and Hades were thrown into the lake of fire. This is the second death, the lake of fire. And if anyone's name was not found written in the book of life, he was thrown into the lake of fire. (Rev. 20:11–15, NASB)

The day is coming when all of those outside of Christ will stand before God and give an account to God for their life. This final judgment is called the "great white throne judgment." Many scoff at the idea of divine judgment, or that there is an everlasting punishment, but Scripture teaches that there is a day coming when all unbelievers, small and great, will stand before God and give an account of themselves. Using *The Preacher's Outline and Sermon Bible*, a verse-by-verse analysis of Rev. 20:11–15 will serve to focus attention on the revelation of the second death. Rev. 20:11.

The place of final judgment is the great white throne of God and those outside of Christ (unbelievers, wicked) will stand there seeing exactly what John saw. They will know that they should never have rejected the Lord Jesus, which is the only way to be made acceptable to God (Heb. 2:3, 12:25).

The throne is white (emphasizing the purity, holiness, and righteousness of God). None of us are perfect and all of us deserve to stand there, but by having Jesus as our Savior and His blood washing away our sin, we are made perfect in the eyes of Father God (Col. 2:26–28; Heb. 10:14–15).

The time of the judgment will be when the heavens and the earth are no longer (either no longer as we know them, or the present heavens and earth are destroyed). Visualize the dismay and shock when they stand before God in a spiritual world, and there is no place found for them. All those outside of Christ have no home, land, possessions; all is gone. Yet there is a place prepared for them (Isa. 34:4, 65:17).

Everyone who stands before God at the great white throne will stand there bearing his or her own sins. Not a single unbeliever will have trusted the blood of Jesus to make them righteous before God; therefore, they are not righteous in the eyes of God. God has a specified eternal place for all unbelievers and wicked people, all clearly outside of Christ.

Revelation 20:12

This Scripture teaches that all human beings will be judged: ordinary, average people, notable men and women, all unbelievers who have ever lived will be judged and given an eternal sentence. No unbeliever is exempt, overlooked, or missed, but all will be called forward by name to face Him who sits on the throne (Rom. 2:16, 14:10; Mt. 18:23). Every unbeliever will have his or her day in the great tribunal of Jehovah God (Rom. 2:6; Mt. 12:36; Rev. 14:12; I Pet. 4:30).

At the great white throne, books will be opened. There are two types of books at this judgment. The first is the book of life. It contains the name of every person who has ever lived. God wants every person to live with Him in heaven throughout eternity, but when a person fails to make Jesus Christ his Savior, their name is blotted out and they are disqualified from being a citizen of heaven (Ex. 32:32–33; Ps. 69:28; Lk. 10:20; Ph. 4:3; Rev. 13:8, 20:15).

The second book is the book of records. This book is the record of all the works of unbelievers. When a person's name is not found in the book of life, because their name has been blotted out, then the book of records is opened, and the person is judged from there.

The first book, the book of life, reveals whether a person will reside in heaven. The second book, the book of records, records everything done by a person (secret sins, grudges, actual deeds, or refusal to help, etc.) and will be used to assess the level of punishment. All those not found in the book of life will be cast into the lake of fire, but punishment—their levels of suffering—will be different. Some will have a very different level of punishment than the petty thief. Both are cast into hell and ultimately the lake of fire, but both will not suffer the same amount of punishment. (See Mt. 11:22–23; Lk. 12:47–48; Ps. 62:12; Jer. 17:10; Mt; 16:27; Lk. 12:48.)

The reality of the great white throne judgment is this: being "good" in this life is not the issue for everlasting life. People will not be judged on the basis of all the good things they have done. Being good can take a person straight to hell as a martin bird to his gourd and ultimately to the lake of fire. Why? Because the person who was being good is not perfect—never has been and never will be. Perfection is found in Jesus Christ. The blood Jesus shed on the cross separates us from our sin and places us in Christ, where we are perfect in the eyes of Father God. (See Heb. 13:20, 21.)

If we reject the blood of Jesus washing away our sins, we also reject the *only* method by which God makes us perfect, and we reject the *only* way by which God accepts our good works. The New Living Translation of Ephesians 2:10 makes the point about acceptable works crystal clear:

"For we are God's masterpiece. He has created us anew in Christ Jesus to do good works which God prepared in advance for us to do." [71]

If a person wants eternal life, and only perfection will afford that eternal life, then the person must look to Jesus. It's the old Christian adage, "Look and live." While the Hebrews were wandering in the wilderness, weary from a long march around the land of Edom and again murmuring against what God had done for them, God sent a plague of fiery serpents to punish them for their unending murmuring (Num. 21:5–9). God responded to their pleas for healing by instructing Moses to create a bronze replica of the serpent and place it on a pole. Moses told the people that if they would look to the bronze serpent, they would live. In John 3:14–15, John declares the serpent on the pole to be a type of Christ. He wrote, "As Moses lifted up the serpent in the wilderness, even so must the Son of Man be lifted up; so that whosoever believes in Him will have eternal life" (NSAB). The secret to personal salvation from sin, the secret to being made perfect, is still "Look and live." [72] Good works are not the issue at the great white throne judgment; the issue is that the blood of Jesus has been rejected or used in name only.

Romans 20:13

The Scripture makes it clear that there is a resurrection for judgment. The first resurrection, which is the resurrection of the righteous,

---

71 New Living Translation, Eph. 2:10, biblehub.com/ephesians/2-10.htm
72 Judson Cornwall, *Back to Basics*, p. 34.

had taken place at least one thousand years earlier.[73] That was the resurrection of the believers (Rev. 20:5–6). The second and final resurrection is the resurrection of all the unbelievers.

The resurrected unbelievers will come from various places, but all will be raised. The dead unbelievers will come from the seas. There is nobody ever lost in the sea that will not come forth. The grave (death) will give up its unbelievers. Every place on the earth or under the sea, even those whose remains were placed in outer space, will be called forth for their proper resurrection appointment. The resurrected unbelievers will stand before God at the great white throne (Rev. 20:13).

---

73 Daniel 12:2 summarizes the two different fates facing humankind: "Many of those who sleep in the dust of the ground will awake, these to everlasting life, but the others to disgrace and everlasting contempt." Everyone will be raised from the dead, but everyone will not have the same destiny. The New Testament reveals separate fates for the just and the unjust. Revelation 20:4–6 identifies the first resurrection and calls those raised "blessed and holy" (Rev. 20:6). The first resurrection is the raising of all believers. It corresponds with Jesus' teaching on the resurrection of the just (righteous) and to "resurrection of life" (Jn. 5:29).

The first resurrection takes place in stages: first Jesus Himself (the "firstfruits," I Cor. 15:20), then the resurrection of the Jerusalem saints (Mt. 27:52–53). Yet to come is the resurrection of "the dead in Christ," at the Lord's return (rapture) (I Thess. 4:16), and resurrection of the martyrs at the end of the Tribulation (Rev. 20:4).

Revelation 20:12–13 identifies those making up the second resurrection as the wicked judged by God at the great white throne judgment prior to being cast into the lake of fire. The second resurrection then is the raising of the unbelievers and the wicked (those outside of Christ); the second resurrection is connected to the second death. It corresponds with Jesus' teaching of the "resurrection of judgment" (Jn. 5:29).

The event that separates the first and the second resurrection seems to be the millennial kingdom. The last of the righteous are raised to reign "with Christ a thousand years" (Rev. 20:4), but the "rest of the dead [that is, the wicked] lived not again until the thousand years were finished." (GotQuestions.org, "What Is the First Resurrection? What Is the Second Resurrection?" www.gotquestions.org/resurrection-first-second.html (quoted, excerpted, amended).

When the unbelievers stand before God at the great white throne judgment, they will be judged according to their works and they will be treated with perfect justice and equity. Bearing their own sin, the unbelievers will:

- Bear a punishment that is equal to their works,
- Bear a punishment that perfectly matches their behavior, and
- Bear a punishment that measures out exactly to what they did.

There is no unfair treatment, discrimination, partiality, or favoritism shown at the great white throne judgment (II Tim 4:1, II Peter 2:9).

Revelation 20:14, 15

Now we come to the complete revelation of what happens to the wicked. It is that hell and death are thrown into the lake of fire, the eternal place of torment where all outside of Christ will be cast. The fire is real; it is not a symbol for anything. It is part of the nature of eternal punishment (Mt. 13:41, 42, 49-50, 25:30).

In times past, in evangelistic fervor, the preacher would ask the congregation why they accepted Jesus as their Savior. Any motive for coming to salvation in Jesus that was outside of love for Jesus was regarded as inferior. These well-meaning evangelists overstated themselves; no one needs to feel diminished. It is a smart, insightful, and wise thing to take steps to avoid the fires of hell and ultimately the second death, which occurs by being cast into the lake of fire. Solomon wrote, "The way of life is above to the wise, that he may depart from hell beneath" (Proverbs 15:24, Torrey's Topical Textbook, AKJV). [74] It is a wise step to come to the salvation of Jesus to avoid hell and the lake of fire.

The reason that a person is cast into the lake of fire is solely, and only, because his or her name is not found in the book of life (Rev. 20:15). The person must possess the perfect life of Jesus if he or she is to have everlasting life in heaven with God. If a person does not possess the perfect life of Christ, then that person, no matter how good, is doomed to go to hell and in the future suffer the second death of being cast into the lake of fire for

---

74 "Hell, the Wise Avoid," bibleapps.com/ttt/h/hell—the_wise_avoid.htm

eternity. No wonder Jesus warned us by saying, "Do not fear those who kill the body but are unable to kill the soul; but rather fear Him who is able to destroy both soul and body in Hell" (Mt. 10:28, NASB). [75]

Chapter Conclusion

Perhaps Jesus spoke so distinctively about hell because He understood its punishment is beyond unbearable, yet the damned soul bears it, and though hell is temporary, its punishment continues eternally in the lake of fire. All inhabitants of hell are destined for the lake of fire, where punishment is eternal (Isa. 33:14, 66:24; Rev. 14:10, 11, 20:10, 15; Rev. 21:8).

The Bible's doctrine of hell uses many synonyms that describe the tortures of hell, and can be expected in the lake of fire because that is the second and final hell:

- Unquenchable fire (Mt. 3:12)
- Outer darkness (Mt. 23:13)
- The blackness of darkness (Jude 13)
- Furnace of fire (Mt. 13:42)
- Torment "in fire and brimstone" (Rev. 14:11)
- "The smoke of their torment" (Rev. 14:11)
- The "place prepared for the Devil and his angels" (Mt. 25:41)
- "Where the worm dieth not and the fire is not quenched" (Mk. 9:44, 46–48)

Specifically we can isolate the following to the lake of fire:
- Satan, the beast (antichrist figure) and the false prophet of Revelation (Rev. 13:11–17) will be cast into the lake of fire (Rev. 20:10).

---

75 For other warnings to take active steps to avoid hell, thus subsequent punishment in the lake of fire, see Matthew 13:41–42, 18:8–9; Luke 25:5; II Thessalonians 1:9; II Peter 2:9; and Psalm 11:6. Additionally, the verse analysis of Revelation 20:11–15 has been drawn and excerpted from *The Preacher's Outline and Sermon Bible*, vol. 2, pp. 1285-1291.

- The lake of fire is the second and final Gehenna, and it is the second death (Rev. 20:14–15).
- Whoever is not found written in the book of life will be cast into the lake of fire (Rev. 20:15).
- The lake of fire is permanent (Jude 12–13).

Just as the blessings of the righteous are eternal, so the punishments of those outside of Christ are eternal. The reason punishment is eternal is that punishment cannot erase the guilt and bring sin to its conclusion. That uniquely remains the work of Jesus on the cross, and in Jesus our sins are washed away from us completely (Mt. 26:28), so eternal punishment is never an issue for the Christian who, if there is time remaining in this life, demonstrates his commitment to Christ by his good works (James 2:14–26).[76]

The account of the lake of fire has brought to an end to the answer of what will happen to the wicked, to those "outside Christ". First, all the dead descend into Sheol/hades (Job 7:7–10, 21:7–13; Psalm 49:7–14). Second, those outside of Christ (the wicked) come to awareness immediately and the sufferings of hell begin (Lk. 16:23; Rev. 20:13). Third, the wicked will stand before God at the great white throne judgment, where they will be judged (assessed a level of suffering) based on their works (Rev. 20:11–15), because the names of those outside of Christ are not written in the book of life. Finally, at the judgment, those outside of Christ are permanently cast into the lake of fire (Rev. 20:15). What a tragedy, and so unnecessary!

---

[76] Those who make a deathbed confession, as we can metaphorically say of the thief on the cross, have no time to live out their surrender to the Lordship of Christ, but it is still accepted by God (Lk. 23:43).

Additionally, the laborer in the vineyard parable (Mt. 20:1–16), where the laborers hired at the end of the day received the same wages as those who worked all day long, proves this point. Yes, God hears and receives the deathbed confession. Not all who come to Christ will have time to live out their surrender to Christ, but their faith has made them "accepted" in the beloved (Eph. 1:6).

Chapter Six

Hell Is Not Culturally Popular

Chapter Introduction

I am aware as I have written this book on hell that this is not a popular topic. Yet, because of its reality, people need to be warned of its existence to provide a divine encouragement to surrender to Christ as Savior and implement scriptural living as applied to their lives by the Holy Spirit.

We see today that the pulpit severely curtails the preaching of this topic. On the website Preaching Today, the top ten downloaded sermons for 2011, which were used or adapted in the pulpit, said nothing about the topic of hell.[77]

In the August 1, 2009, *USA Today* article titled "Many Americans Don't Believe in Hell, but What about Pastors?," Greg Garrison reports on the Birmingham, Alabama, Samford University's Beeson Divinity School's recent annual pastors school. Kurt Sellers, the director of the Global Center at Samford University, led four workshops to discuss "Whatever happened to hell?" He asked how many pastors had "ever" preached a sermon on hell. "Nobody had," Garrison reported. Then Sellers offered this editorial comment: "I think it's something people want to avoid, and I understand why. It's a difficult topic."

The Reverend Fred Johns, the pastor of Brookview Wesleyan Church in Irondale, Alabama, said, after a workshop discussing hell, that pastors do shy away from the topic of everlasting damnation. "It's out of fear

---

[77] See Preaching Today's "Top Ten Sermons of 2011," preachingtoday.com.

we'll not appear relevant," Johns said. "It's pressure from the culture to not speak anything negative. I think we've begun to deny hell. There's an assumption that everybody's going to make it to heaven somehow." Then Sellers hesitated. "The soft sell on hell reflects an increasingly market-conscious approach...Jesus never soft-pedaled the concept of hell."[78] The revelation of hell swims in opposition to culture, and all who maintain its reality can sense that. What has happened to us, so that in the West we shun such a revelation? "The Scriptures clearly teach that every person born on this earth will go to an eternal place where he or she will be assigned an eternal position. God, who founded eternity and created all creatures of time, tells us in His Word that there are only two places where persons will dwell eternally. The first is heaven and the second is hell." [79]

Using the thought of Frances Schaeffer as a guide, this chapter will investigate how we have arrived at a point of cultural resistance to the topic of hell, and in reality, all biblical absolutes. That will give us context for what we face. Then proposals will be made as to how this topic may be kept relevant among ourselves and among those we influence.

THE PURSUIT OF FREEDOM

One of my favorite devices when preaching a funeral sermon for someone (I did that frequently in the thirty-one years I pastored) was to overview the changes that occurred during the deceased's lifespan and report on how the deceased navigated his or her way through those differences. Since the 1960s, a cataclysmic shift in culture has taken place in the USA, whether it is coming from the law or government, or whether it

---

78 Greg Garrison, *USA Today*, "Many Americans Don't Believe in Hell, but What about Pastors?," usatoday30.usatoday.com/news/religion/2009-08-01.hell..., August 1, 2009.

79 Cornwall, *Back to Basics*, p. 310.

is happening in our schools, our local communities, or in our families… our culture has been submerged and lost, and largely thrown away.[80]

Schaeffer notes that morality has been "turned on its head with every form of moral perversion being praised and glorified in the media and the world of entertainment."[81] So how do we make sense of what has happened? To answer that question, Schaeffer looks to an October 1983 article by Roger Rosenblatt in *Time* magazine titled "What Really Mattered?" The article argues that the polarizing idea of our age has been freedom. Not just freedom as an abstract ideal, but freedom in an absolute sense.

> To be free was to be modern…The American twentieth century was to be the century of unleashing, of breaking away at first from the 19th century (as Freud, Proust, Einstein, and others had done), and eventually from any restraint at all.[82]

As the article progresses, *Time* magazine opines that "limits were intrinsically evil."[83]

According to Schaeffer, we inherited from the Reformation a strong emphasis upon Christian truth, which provided the necessary foundation for a healthy freedom to exist. Abandonment of reformation principles has brought about a restless search for freedom devoid of any restraint. Therein lies a major catalyst that has introduced much change into the American culture.

The Reformation not only brought forth the clear preaching of the gospel, it also gave shape to society as a whole. It is not that every one of the Reformation countries was truly Christian, but through the

---

80 Frances Schaeffer, *The Complete Works of Frances Schaeffer, A Christian Worldview*, vol. 4: *The Great Evangelical Disaster*, Crossiamy Books, Westchester, IL, 1982, p. 307.
81 Schaeffer, *The Great Evangelical Disaster*, pp. 307-308.
82 Roger Rosenblatt, "What Really Mattered?" *Time*, October (60th Anniversary Issue), 1983, p. 25.
83 Rosenblatt, p. 26.

Reformation, a biblical worldview and biblical knowledge were disseminated through the culture. "The freedoms which grew out of this were tremendous; and yet with the forms [government, law, entertainment, social morality, ethics, etc.] grounded in a Biblical consensus or ethos, the freedom did not lead to chaos."[84] At the time of the Reformation, the large majority of people believed in basic Christian truths such as the existence of God, that Jesus is the son of God, that there is an afterlife, that morality is concerned with what is truly right and wrong (as opposed to relative morality), that God will punish those who do wrong, that there truly is evil in the world as a result of the fall, and that the Bible truly is God's word. In the Reformation countries (northern Europe), most people believed those things. [85]

This vast dissemination of biblical knowledge can correctly be identified as a "biblical consensus," a "Christian consensus," or a "Christian ethos." It is correct to hold the opinion that this biblical consensus decidedly influenced the culture of the Reformation countries and the extensions of those countries in North America, Australia, and New Zealand, without looking to any age as the "golden age." The northern European countries of the Reformation and the extension of these countries (such as the United States) brought about a Christian consensus that profoundly shaped the cultures, bringing forth many blessings across the spectrum of society.[86]

But something has happened in my lifetime, beginning in the 1960s. The freedoms that were founded upon a biblical consensus, a Christian consensus and ethos, has now morphed into an autonomous freedom (a self-governing, independent-from-God freedom). The freedom insisted upon today, in the former Reformation-influenced countries, is being cut loose from all constraints of biblical consensus and ethos. This pursuit of freedom, with humanity setting itself up as God, which defies the knowledge of God and His moral directives, has become the world spirit

---

84 Schaeffer, *What Really Matters?*, vol. 4, p. 300.
85 Schaeffer, *What Really Matters?*, vol. 4, p. 416.
86 Schaeffer, *What Really Matters?*, vol. 4, pp. 416-417.

of this age. Back in its October 1983 issue, *Time* magazine had it right: the idea that has characterized our age has been the idea of freedom, but it is a freedom free of any constraints at all.

This is the reason we have breakdowns in society (Wall Street greed, morals redefined, misuse of the educational system and government calling good evil and evil good). Our society has pursued freedom, without biblical constraint. Naturally, this forbids the preaching and teaching of eternal punishment in hell and the lake of fire, for to admit judgment, a society must admit that there are biblical absolutes. The Christian ethos is what the former Reformation countries have abandoned since the upheaval of the 1960s. (It can be argued that abandonment of Christian principles was occurring decades before.)

WE WRESTLE NOT AGAINST FLESH AND BLOOD

The world spirit of this age—the pursuit of freedom from any constraint—continues to roll forward pulverizing all that we hold dear in its path. Man sets himself up, indifferent to God-given morals and spiritual truth, and he himself becomes the force of destruction that leads to the breakdown of the culture. "And when this happens, there really are very few alternatives, all morality becomes relative, law becomes arbitrary, and society moves forward to disintegration."[87]

This destruction of culture is not the working of flesh and blood but of principalities and powers. To our shame, few Christians have recognized that satanic influences stand behind the world spirit of this age. Bible-believing Christians are locked in a battle of cosmic proportions. We are in a life-and-death struggle for the minds and hearts of people that has real implication for this life and eternity.

One of the most attention-grabbing teachings of the Bible is the issue of hell and the everlasting lake of fire. Its revelation is designed to arrest

---

87 Schaeffer, *What Really Matters?*, p. 310.

sinful behavior and bring about surrender to Jesus'ss salvation. Yet, the truth about eternal punishment is deemphasized today. "The subject is repugnant to the human mind, yet no subject is of greater importance."[88] Satan uses the pursuit of freedom without constraint to infiltrate and decimate cultures.

WHY THE PULPIT SHOULD PREACH ABOUT HELL AND THE LAKE OF FIRE

It is our duty as faithful ministers of Jesus Christ to preach the whole counsel of God. If the pulpit doesn't warn people, we are not fulfilling all the roles that the Holy Spirit has called us to fulfill. Princeton theologian A. A. Hodges tells us, "As Christians we have had scriptures for almost twenty centuries. We read that 'all the great church fathers, reformers, and historical churches with their recensions, and translations of the sacred scriptures, their liturgies and hymns; all the great evangelical theologians and biblical scholars, with their grammars, dictionaries, commentaries, and classical systems have uniformly agreed in their understanding of the teaching of the sacred scriptures as to the endlessness of the future sufferings of all who die impenitent. And this has come to pass against the universal and impetuous current of human fears and sympathies.'" [89]

Regardless of the cultural pushback, the faithful minister will preach the whole counsel of God, even the subjects that are not popular. God unequivocally proclaims through the prophet Ezekiel, "I take no pleasure in the death of the wicked, but rather that the wicked turn from his way and live..." (Ezk. 33:11, NASB). The faithful minister must proclaim the truth about hell and the lake of fire to warn his or her listeners of the wrath to come.

---

88 D. James Kennedy, *Why I Believe*, World Publishing, Dallas, TX, 1980, p. 70.

89 A. A. Hodge, *Popular Lectures on Theological Themes* (Philadelphia, Presbyterian Board of Publications, 1887), pp. 456–457.

It is a shame that in our era, which is experiencing a greater display of satanic influence than in past eras, that the Christian church does not understand who our real enemy is. Satan is behind the world spirit that agitates for freedom without constraints.

Humanity has been the unwitting servant to an invisible, perversely intelligent, deceitful, powerful, and heartless master who is the god of this world (II Cor. 4:4). He has defiled cultures by appealing to our self-centered natures. He has corrupted music, literature, art, and religion. He has enslaved our minds by appealing to the desires of the flesh and of the eyes and the pride of life (I Jn. 2:16). He confuses us by hiding or shading the truth, distorting reality, denying absolutes, emphasizing vanity, and making available such varied opinions that different philosophies, worldviews, and ways of life are standard fare.[90] It is clear to those that have eyes to see that Satan, the god of this world, may bring ridicule to any minister preaching the reality of eternal punishment. The pulpit needs to thunder with the truth that those outside of Christ will go into an endless punishment: hell temporarily, then eternally into the lake of fire. It is not contrary to rationality, and faithfulness demands that the subject of eternal punishment be taught and preached with conviction.

The Apostle John wrote that "the whole world lies in the power of the evil one (I Jn. 5:19b, NASB). So we must expect resistance to the truth about eternal punishment and to biblical absolutes that do not fit a culture that is agitating for freedom without constraint.

Standing against culture is hard and may well be costly. Yet, we have the biblical example of righteous people (for example, Noah) who stood for the truth of God against culture. In his work, *Death in the City*, author Francis Schaeffer investigates the life of Jeremiah and how he bravely withstood culture.

---

90   John W. Rittenbaugh, BibleTools, "Satan" (forerunner commentary), "After Pentecost, Then What," undated.

Jeremiah Prophesied in an Age Similar to Ours

Jeremiah was called the "weeping prophet," for we see him crying over the people and the culture that had turned away from God.

Jeremiah was born in Anathoth (Jer. 1:1) and he died in Egypt, probably in his sixties. He did not have an easy life. His message was not an easy message. He stands as an example of faithfulness that brought hard and unfavorable consequences. The Lord made it clear that his message would be poorly received by a culture in revolt.

"Now behold, I have made you today as a fortified city and as a pillar of iron and as walls of bronze against the whole land…they will fight against you, but they will not overcome you, for I am with you to deliver you" (Jer. 1:18-19, NASB).

So today, former Reformation countries will resist the preaching of hell and the lake of fire. They logically resist the preaching of punishment because the culture has drifted from many of its Christian restraints. To accept the truth of eternal punishment is to admit biblical truth and recognize our variances from that eternal truth and that our culture will not do. Like Jeremiah, those who teach and preach the existence of hell and the lake of fire will be met with derision, resistance, and even hostility. Ministers and lay Christians who are looking for an easy life in this post-Christian culture are not being realistic. It was not so in Jeremiah's day, nor is it true today.

Jeremiah, in his book, will analyze the ways in which his culture was turning from the Lord. He acknowledges that there was much religion in the culture, but the religion did not please the Lord. He would write, "For what purpose does frankincense come to me from Sheba, and the sweet cane from a distant land? Your burnt offerings are not acceptable. And your sacrifices are not pleasing to me" (Jer. 6:20, NASB). There was plenty of sacrifice and incense, but God was not pleased.

If we choose to update this message from God, would we hear Him saying, "For what purpose is your beautiful facility and its beautiful interior design, when there has not been a faithfulness to preach the whole counsel of the Bible? Your giving is not acceptable to me, and your sacrificial giving does not please me"? It is paramount that the pulpit and the lecturer bring the whole truth of God and eternity, not avoid the truth of hell, the lake of fire, and eternal punishment. Through Jeremiah God is saying that more external religion means nothing to Him. God wants His truth to be revealed by His church that is acting above reproach.

As Schaeffer noted, "We need new John Bunyans to point out what occurs when men turn to Vanity Fair."[91] When we do not hear the whole truth of God, the culture is destroyed, and ultimately society is destroyed. God said of Jerusalem, using the capital city to illustrate that the culture and society of Israel had turned from them, "I will make Jerusalem a heap of ruins, a haunt of jackals; and I will make the cities of Judah a desolation" (Jer. 9:11, NASB). Until we hear the prophecy and teaching of eternal punishment in hell and the lake of fire, the church will not be effective to see the hearts of men turn and surrender.[92]

Our generation needs to be told the truth of hell and the lake of fire. Our generation needs to be told that humanity cannot disregard God and to do so is to stand under the judgment of God, in this life and in the

---

91 Schaeffer, *Death in the City*, p. 231. Vanity Fair is a place in Bunyan's *Pilgrim's Progress*. It is a fair in the town of Vanity that symbolizes worldly ostentation and frivolity. It goes on perpetually. (See "Vanity Fair," Dictionary.com.)

92 Bible.org reports that Pollster George H. Gallop Jr. says 70 percent of Americans believe most churches and synagogues are not effective in helping people find meaning in life. (Bible.org, "Churches Ineffective." See also *Church Cell* magazine, vol. 1, November 4, p. 4, and the *Houston Chronicle*, August 29, 1992, p. 3E.) According to Dr. Richard. J. Krejeir in "Statistics and Reasons for Church Decline," half of all US churches added no new members in 2007 (see www.churchleadership.org).

David T. Olson, the director of church planting for the Evangelical Covenant Church, surveying only Christian churches (i.e., evangelical mainline and Catholic) states that the percentage of Americans regularly attending church is 18.7 percent. (See "How Many Americans Attend Church Each Week?" Justin Taylor, "thegospelcoalition.org," March 1, 2007.) America needs the church to preach the arresting message of eternal punishment in hell and the lake of fire.

next. It is not a popular or easy message, but strong, godly ministers like Jeremiah go before us as an example that we are to be faithful to God and warn this society to flee the wrath to come.

Chapter Conclusion

The first five chapters of this book answered the question "What will happen to those who finish this life outside of Christ?" To answer that question, the gradual revelation of hell was examined from Job through the Book of Revelation, which concluded with the revelation of the lake of fire. What will happen to those who finish this life "outside of Christ" is horrible; therefore it is incumbent upon on the church to warn humanity to flee the coming wrath by surrendering their hearts to Jesus. Yet the church is practically silent about the eternal horror awaiting those who do not know Jesus as their Savior.

It is accurate to say, as has been said for several decades, that we live in a post-Christian culture. Having turned from the knowledge given by God, the culture is secularized and is now ambivalent or even hostile to biblical truth. Think for a moment about the hostility the culture has toward those who support creationism as opposed to evolution as a way to explain the development of life on planet Earth. The Christian influence on the culture has been greatly diminished from what it was in the beginning of the 1960s (before the student revolts). Ours is a post-Christian culture, and there is no longer a consensus or Christian ethos in our society. The United States is the living picture of Romans 1:21, 22:

> For even though they knew God, they did not honor him as God or give thanks, but they became futile in their speculations, and their foolish heart was darkened. Professing to be wise, they became fools. (NASB)

For our culture to turn from biblical truth to manmade ideas is very unwise and even foolish. The Scriptures teach that we have become fools. Bent on the pursuit of freedom from any constraint, especially from

God's truth and moral absolutes—our culture has set itself on the path of self-destruction. A part of this path is the ignoring of, even denial of, external punishment in hell and the lake of fire. Voices in our day cry to be free to kill the child in the womb, voices cry to execute children in utero that do not quite measure up to expected standards, voices cry to be free to abandon the spouse and the family, voices cry to marry a person of the same gender, and voices cry to be free of judgment. Therefore, the truth of eternal punishment is ignored or suppressed by the church, because culture will push back. [93]

Nevertheless, we are not excused from standing for biblical truth. When the church does not speak against the prevailing sins of the post-Christian world and emphasize eternal punishment for turning from

---

93 Seeking freedom without restraint has undercut the Christian consensus in our society. Christianity once had a powerful influence over culture in America. The influence of the Enlightenment has been a major reason, but not the only reason, our culture has shifted away from Christianity. The Enlightenment was a movement of thought that began to appear in the mid-seventeenth century; it reached its most clear-cut expression in eighteenth-century Germany. At the end of the nineteenth century, the ideas of the Enlightenment began to have a significant influence upon Christianity in America. In general, the movement emphasized the sufficiency of human reason and skepticism concerning the validity of traditional authority, which included Christian truth. (See F. L. Cross, ed., *The Oxford Dictionary of the Christian Church*, London, Oxford University Press, 1958, pp. 104, 105 for an excellent definition of the Enlightenment.) The Oxford Dictionary definitely could be summarized by saying that the central ideas of the Enlightenment stand in antithesis to Christian truth. The ideas attack God Himself and His character. As a result of the Enlightenment ideas, the reformation ideas were undercut, and the door was open for a headlong variance from biblical truth. These variances were the foundation of what *Time* magazine identified in their fiftieth anniversary edition in 1983 as the "idea [characterizing our age]," of freedom in an absolute sense, freedom without constraint. This pursuit of freedom has changed the culture of America from a Christian ethos to a secular ethos. It started with the Enlightenment and has borne the fruit of an unrestrained pursuit of freedom that is free of any constraint.

God and His Scripture, then we do not follow God's example through Jeremiah who spoke the truth of God.[94] It is an era when backbone needs to be found and the church needs to warn the generations living that there is a coming wrath. We need to proclaim that to escape that wrath, we must flee to the salvation found only in Jesus'ss blood shed on the cross. The Apostle Peter writes:

> Knowing that you were not redeemed with perishable things like silver and gold from your futile way of life inherited from your forefathers, but with precious blood, as a lamb unblemished and spotless, the blood of Christ. (I Pet. 1:18, 19, NASB)

The church in this hour needs to rise and bring eternal truth about hell and the lake of fire.[95] It is an arresting message that will prick the hearts of men, just as did Jonathan Edwards's sermon "Sinners in the Hands of an Angry God." [96]

---

94 Schaeffer, *Death and the City*, "The Message of Judgment," p. 229.

95 Although my dependence upon Frances Schaeffer's thought was acknowledged at the beginning of this chapter, I want to further remind the reader that I have used and excerpted his thought for this chapter.

96 For the text of Jonathan Edwards's sermon, "Sinners in the Hands of an Angry God," see "Voices of Democracy," "Edwards, 'Sinners in the Hands…,' Speech Text" at voicesofdemocracy.umd.edu.

Jonathan Edwards was interrupted many times before finishing the sermon by people moaning and crying out, "What shall I do to be saved?" See Wikipedia, "Sinners in the Hands of an Angry God," en.wikipedia.org. I dare to believe that the church would find similar reactions in multiplied millions if they returned to warning people about eternal damnation for all outside of Christ in hell and the lake of fire.

CHAPTER SEVEN

WHAT DOES IT MEAN TO BE "INSIDE OF CHRIST" AND "OUTSIDE OF CHRIST"?

CHAPTER INTRODUCTION

We now enter the sphere of Christian truth, which has to do with the heart of the Christian message. Christian faith rests solely upon the salvation of Jesus through His blood that was shed upon the cross.[97] It is from our salvation, by the blood of Jesus, that we see and

---

97 Jesus plainly teaches His disciples at the institution of the Lord's Supper (The Eucharist), "For this is my blood of the covenant, which I pour out for many for forgiveness of sins" (Mt. 26:28, NASB). Paul, under the inspiration of the Holy Spirit, writes, "In Him we have redemption through His blood, the forgiveness of our trespasses [sins], according to the riches of His grace" (Ep. 1:7, NASB). He further writes, "In whom we have redemption through His blood, the forgiveness of sin" (Col. 1, 14, NKJV). Unfortunately, I could not quote the Colossian passage from the NASB, for they have erroneously chosen to adopt the NU-Text (NU stands for Nestle—Aland Greek New Testament/United Bible Society. These are texts based on the oldest, but not the most numerous ancient manuscripts.) The Apostle John pens "...Jesus Christ... who loves us and released us from our sins by [or "in"] His blood" (Rev. 1:5, NASB).

gladly embrace the doctrine of creation, the doctrine of last things, the doctrine of redemption and consummation.[98]

This particular chapter is critical to this book. So far we have been consistently asserting that all of those "outside of Christ" will experience the postmortem tragedy of hell and the lake of fire. Therefore, what does it mean to be "in Christ," where there is salvation and dwelling with Father God through eternity, and conversely what does it mean to be "outside of Christ," where there is eternal judgment?

I am aware that the Christian truth of being "outside of Christ" is not popular, but biblical truth must stand as our rule of faith and conduct, for "Heaven and Earth shall pass away, but My words will not pass away" (Lk. 21:33, NASB). When all the vast creation, the earth, and the stars will disappear in their turn, the words of Jesus and the entire Scripture will remain. Therefore we must look to Scripture to see what it means to be "inside Christ" or "outside of Christ."

INSIDE OF CHRIST

The phrase "in Christ" is found multiple times in the New Testament, and the use of this phrase gives us a quick overview of what it means to be "in Christ."

Being "in Christ" means:
1) We are free from condemnation (Rom. 8:1).
2) We are a new creation (II Cor. 5:17; Eph. 2.10; Gal. 6:15).
3) We are reconciled to God (Eph. 2:13).
4) We have liberty (Gal. 2:4).
5) We are blessed with every spiritual blessing (Eph. 1:3).
6) We are a member of the body of Christ (Gal. 3:28; Eph. 3:6).
7) We have a direction (Ph. 3:13–14; Col. 1:28).
8) We have eternal life (I Thess. 4:16).

---

98 Karl Barth, *Church Dogmatics*, vol. IV, "The Doctrine of Reconciliation," Hendrickson Publishers, Peabody, MA, p. 3.

While there are other Scriptural references to being "in Christ," these assure us of the blessings of forgiveness, intercession, mercy, fellowship, hope, peace, victory, and salvation. Jesus Christ told Nicodemus, "You must be born again" (Jn. 3:7, NASB). Earlier Jesus had asserted imperiously, "Unless one is born again, he cannot see the kingdom of God" (Jn. 3:3, NASB). The new birth occurs by the act of placing our faith in Jesus Christ, plus nothing—this act of faith washes away our sins by His blood shed on the cross, thereby bringing us into the family of God and launching eternal life. The new birth places us "in Christ," and in Him we have all spiritual blessings.

Dr. James Kennedy tells us that "along with John and Charles Wesley, the famous Anglican clergyman, George Whitfield, was much responsible for the transformation of England and the Great Awakening in America. In a letter to Benjamin Franklin, who used to delight to hear Whitfield speak, he said: 'As I find you growing more and more famous in the learned world, I would recommend to your diligent and unprejudiced study the mystery of the new birth. It is a most important study, and, when mastered, will richly answer all your pains. I bid you, my friend, remember that one at whose bar we shall both presently appear hath solemnly declared that without it we shall in no wise see His Kingdom.'" [99] George Whitfield was inviting Benjamin Franklin to be reborn in Christ's salvation, and that would place in him the relationship called "in Christ." [100] In that relationship, Benjamin Franklin would be able to share in and enjoy the good things of God, which the Scripture teaches are found "in Christ." Our acceptance of Jesus as Savior, just

---

99 Dr. James Kennedy, *Why I Believe*, World Publishing, Dallas, TX, 1980, p. 130. Quoted in *Re-Entry* by John Wesley White (Minneapolis: World Wide Publications, 1970), p. 106.

100 Being "in Christ" does not refer to being at a specific physical place, like in the house or the yard. Being "in Christ" refers to being in a relationship where Jesus is our Savior. It is similar to the phrase "in the family," which describes a relationship, not a physical location. (John Quinn, "The Meaning of Being 'In Christ,'" www.bradley-churchofchrist.com/topics/sanctification.htm.)

like the thief on the cross (Lk. 23:39–43), is the moment we are in the relationship that is identified as being "in Christ." Then, in obedience to Lord Jesus, we follow Christ's example of being baptized in water (sprinkling or immersion is not an issue for God, but our humble obedience is), so our relationship of being "in Christ" becomes public. Baptism is such a strong statement of being "in Christ" that Paul writes, "For all of you who were baptized into Christ have clothed yourselves with Christ" (Gal. 3:27, NASB). Our personal surrender to Jesus as our Savior brings us into the relationship identified as "in Christ." Our baptism makes public that we are "in Christ."

Already in this chapter there has been an abbreviated listing of what it means to be "in Christ." Amplifying on the previously mentioned Ephesians 1:3, we see that Paul explains that "in Christ" we are God's "chosen" (verse 5), we are made "holy and blameless" before God (verse 6), we are adopted as the sons [and daughters] of God (verse 5), we have "redemption through His blood and the forgiveness of our trespasses" (verse 7), we have "obtained an inheritance" (verse 11), we have a "hope" and we are "seated in Him with the Holy Spirit" (verse 12). Those blessings come to us only when we are in the relationship identified as "in Christ."

All of those blessings are precious and accrue to those "in Christ." But one of the most distinctive blessings occurs in Ephesians 1:4, when holiness and blamelessness come into our life:

> Cyprian became one of the great leaders in the early church as holiness and blamelessness came into his life from being "in Christ." He was born into a wealthy pagan family of Carthage sometime during the third century (ca. 200 CE). He enjoyed galloping about Carthage in his gold and bejeweled chariot, wearing his fancy clothes studded with diamonds and precious stones, living a life of debauchery. In the early days of his conversion, he wrote a letter (Epistola ad Donatum de gratia Dei) acknowledging his wonder if he could be freed from the life he had lived for so long. (He was 35 years of age before he came to

salvation in Christ and was baptized.) It seemed to him utterly impossible that his life could change. Yet by the help of the new birth that washed away his stain, public baptism in water, a light from above was infused in [his] reconciled heart...The second birth restored [him] to a new man.[101]

Cyprian became the Bishop of Carthage in 249 CE and an important early church author. His skill in Latin rhetoric led to his being considered the preeminent Latin writer in Western Christianity until Jerome (354–430 CE). All of that was possible because of the new birth, which brought him into the relationship identified as "in Christ." [102] Being in Christ brings spiritual blessings.

The reason why being in the "in Christ" relationship is so transformative to all areas of life is because "in Christ," Christ is in us (Col. 1:27). In the early church, one of the people God reached for was Saul of Tarsus. Like Cyprian 150 years after Saul of Tarsus, he was an unlikely tool of divine service.[103]

Saul of Tarsus was not haphazard about his religion; he was zealous to the point of fanaticism, and he became a great persecutor of the

---

101 Wikipedia, "Cyprian," March 2014, quoting Cyprian, ad Donatum, 3-4, en.wikipedia.org/wiki/Cyprian. See also Dr. James Kennedy, "Why I Believe," pp. 134-135.

102 Ibid. James Kennedy notes that many testimonies of a changed life exist, including some very famous people such as William Gladstone, Abraham Lincoln, Fyodor Dostoyevsky, Leo Tolstoy, and others. All changed as a result of the new birth and being in the relationship with Jesus identified as "in Christ."

103 God often finds His workers in usual places and circumstance. Noah was a righteous man in a degenerate and degraded generation. Abraham lived among idolatry in Ur of the Chaldees, Moses was a fugitive who fled into the desert regions of the Sinai, Isaiah was a prophet in the royal court, Ezekiel was a captive in Babylon, Daniel was a government servant in Babylon, Peter was a fisherman on the sea of Galilee, Saul of Tarsus was a Pharisee and a theological graduate who called himself a Hebrew of Hebrews. (Judson Cornwall, *Meeting God*, Creation House, Altamonte Springs, FL, 1986, p. 224).

early Christian church (Acts 9:1, 2). Saul's murderous fanaticism toward Christians was a continuing condition in him. Saul had set in his will to protect God and truth, no matter how damaging to others. No wonder that the disciples in Jerusalem considered Saul of Tarsus public enemy number one. But God had selected Saul of Tarsus to replace Judas. In the ninth chapter of Acts, Luke tells us that Paul was converted to Christ. Paul himself will tell the story in Acts 22 and 29. His conversion was instantaneous, but he progressively became more like Jesus inside the relationship of being "in Christ."

Saul had long known the name of Jesus, but after seeing and hearing Jesus on the Damascus Road, he would learn the truth and nature of the Lord Jesus. Indeed, Saul acknowledged to Agrippa, twenty-five years after his conversion, that he was blind to Christ before he met Jesus (Acts 26:9–20).

Saul, renamed Paul, was converted, and though he did not yet acknowledge or understand it, he came into the "in Christ" relationship. In that relationship, Paul will extol the stature of Jesus. He will write of Jesus, "If you confess with your mouth Jesus as Lord and believe in your heart that God raised Him from the dead, you shall be saved" (Rom. 10:9, NASB). His theologically trained mind was being redirected by the Holy Spirit into the truths of Christ.

During the long and agonizing years of solitude Paul spent in the desert area of Sinai, as he reflected on the Scriptures, he developed a threefold theism that explains what it means to be in Christ. We are in Christ, Christ is in us corporately, and Christ is in us individually.[104] While on Mars Hill, Paul explained the first revelatory concept of his three-part theism. He said, "For in Him we live and move and exist." Thus, Paul moved God out of a manmade temple into the world as its creator and preserver and established that He is everywhere, present, and not far from any of us. Paul saw that our lives needed Christ's activity, so he says "in Him we live and move." Paul's inspired revelation is one portion of what it means to be "in Christ": we are in Him. The New

---

104 Judson Cornwall, *Meeting God*, p. 235.

Testament uses the expression "in Christ" 164 times. So for those who are redeemed by Jesus's blood, they can know that everywhere they go, He is already there; that is a part of being "in Christ." [105]

Paul's second concept is that Christ is in the lives of the believers corporately. Paul had come to understand that redeemed humankind has a very personal involvement with Jehovah through Jesus, and Paul saw that Jesus dwells in believers collectively.

As Paul understands God's revelation of Christ in us collectively, Paul sees it expressed in these ways: Christ in His family (Eph. 2:19; Rom 8:16, 17; Eph. 3:14, 15, 16; II Cor. 6:16; Eph. 2:21, 22) and Christ in His church (Col. 1:18, 24; I Cor. 12:27).

Then we come to the third part of the revelation that shows us what it means to be "in Christ"… "Christ in You" (Col. 1:27). The phrase "Christ in You" is God's revelation to Paul that believers have Christ in them, His presence and person living in us believers.

Although most translators agree that the Greek preposition used in the phrase— "en"—needs to be translated as "in," signifying that Christ dwells within the hearts of individual believers by His Spirit, the real emphasis is on the word "you." Paul reveals that Christ dwells in "you" (Col. 1:27; Gal. 14:19; II Thess. 1:10). Christianity is Christ in our heart. That is why Paul prayed for the Ephesians "that Christ may dwell in your hearts through faith" (Eph. 3:17), and he stated, "Christ lives in me" (Gal. 2:20), and he asked the Corinthian believers, "Do you not know yourselves that Jesus Christ is in you?" (II Cor. 13:5). [106]

That is what it means to be "in Christ." We come into a relationship with Christ at salvation, and that relationship is identified as being "in Christ." It changes us completely because we gradually take on the personality of Christ. The overarching explanation of what it means to be in Christ is given to us by Paul's threefold revelation: We are in Christ, Christ is in us corporately, and Christ is in us individually. [107]

---

105 Ibid., pp. 225-237.
106 Judson Cornwall, *Meeting God*.
107 Ibid., pp. 238-243.

OUTSIDE OF CHRIST

Paul Tillich[108] in volume three of his magnum opus, *Systematic Theology*, observes that "no one can stand the threat of eternal death either for himself or for others; yet the threat cannot be dismissed…" [109] To address that threat, attempts have been made to overcome its definitiveness both inside and outside of Christianity. Three attempts are important to acknowledge: reincarnation, purgatory, and the intermediary state. "All three express the feeling that one cannot make the moment of death decisive for man's ultimate destiny." [110] In the case of infants, children, and undeveloped adults, there is no issue; in Tillich's words, "this would be a complete absurdity," meaning that they do not possess the capacity to acknowledge Christ as Savior, nor does Father

---

108 Paul Tillich (1886–1965) was a German American Christian Lutheran existentialist philosopher and theologian. He is widely recognized as one of the most influential theologians of the twentieth century. Among the general public, he is best known for his works *The Courage to Be* (1952) and *Dynamics of Faith* (1957). Theologically, Tillich is best known for his three-volume work *Systematic Theology* (1951–63). See Wikipedia, Paul Tillich (en.wikipedia.org/wiki/Paul_Tillich).
109 Paul Tillich, *Systematic Theology*, vol. 3, The University of Chicago Press, Chicago, IL, p. 416.
110 Tillich, p. 416.

God expect that of those three groups.[111] However, in the case of mature people, the three attempts to extend a decision about eternity to beyond death disregards the biblical truth that death terminates the opportunity for any further decisions about eternity. Our decision about eternal salvation is fixed at death.

Several biblical passages clearly present that the Bible teaches that everyone will die and be judged for works done in this life (Heb. 9:27) and that each person's eternal destiny, either reward or condemnation,

---

111   Randy Alcorn, author of the lengthy Internet article, "Do Infants Go to Heaven When They Die?," is helpful here (see Randy Alcorn, "Do Infants Go to Heaven When They Die," www.epm.org/.../Jan/5/do-infants-go-to-heaven-when-they-die).

Alcorn states that 99 percent of the evangelical community believes in infant salvation (I do too, and so does Alcorn). Scripture makes no reference to an age of accountability, nor does it seem to imply that there *is* an age of accountability. The huge problem is Romans 3 and all the "depravity" passages. The teaching of Scripture is that we are conceived sinners (Ps. 51:5) and born sinners (Ps. 58:3), and to be a sinner is to be outside of Christ, therefore lost and unqualified to enter heaven.

So, if children are saved, it cannot be because of innocence—they are not innocent, but conceived sinners and born sinners. For any person to be saved, it must be through the work of Christ (I Tim. 2:5), and unless someone is born again, he or she cannot enter the kingdom of God, but an infant cannot choose Christ. So what do we see to address this? First, the "age of accountability" is not a biblical teaching (it is not unbiblical, but abiblical). So, God in His mercy and special love for infants and children covers them with the blood of Jesus. Jesus specifically states about children: "For the Kingdom of Heaven belongs to such as these" (Mt. 19:14, NASB). Additionally, the infilling of John the Baptist with the Holy Spirit while in Elizabeth's womb is an example of God regarding a righteousness to infants and children (Lk. 1:15). And the strongest argument used for infant salvation is David's statement about his infant son who died (II Sam. 12:23)—David in his personal agony was consoling himself with the belief that he would join his son in the presence of God.

As to children and underdeveloped adults, the same character of God presides. They are not able; God doesn't expect them to proclaim Jesus as Savior if they are not able, so God does right and covers them in the blood of Jesus (Gen. 18:25).

will be based on what was done in this life (Mt. 7:21–23, 13:36–43; Jn. 5:28-29). Jesus's teaching of Lazarus and the rich man showed that the rich man had no anticipation he would ever be delivered from the flames and the reason he was there was because of the works he did/did not do in his earthly life (Lk. 16:19–31). Finally, the great white throne judgment in Revelation 20:11–15 without question bases eternal destiny on our works done in this life. The Scripture is totally silent on whether there will be a salvation opportunity after death.[112] All who choose to be "in Christ" must do so prior to death.

God has placed within human beings the desire for eternity. Solomon writes, "He has also set eternity in their heart…" (Ecc. 3:11, NASB). God has put into the heart and mind of human beings a notion of infinity, of duration, and humans want to connect positively to eternity. Positive connection to eternity happens only by coming to Father God through the blood of Jesus. Thus the three efforts to overcome the truth that death is the end of a salvation opportunity only introduces confusion and profound ambiguity into the matter of eternal salvation. The idea of the reincarnation of individual lives has great power over roughly 24 percent of American adults,[113] and it is estimated that "about a quarter of the world's population believes in reincarnation in some form."[114] It is seen as a way of connecting to eternity with life beyond death. But this not a consoling idea because the negative character of life in reincarnation. It is a painful way to connect to eternity. But the difficulty of reincarnation is that there is no way to experience the subject's identity in different incarnations, so it provides no development of the self after death. Reincarnation certainly demonstrates the high desire to connect

---

112 Ronald H. Hash, "Is There Salvation after Death?," www.equip.og/artides/is-there-salvaion-after-death. This article first appeared in the *Christian Research Journal*, vol. 27, number 4 (2004).

113 Prokerala.com, "24 percent of Americans Believe in Reincarnation," www.prokerala.com/mews/articles/a99849.html.

114 Datahookup.com, "Reincarnation Facts and Resources," www.datahookup.com/content-reincarnation-facts-and-....

to eternity and it demonstrates that eternity really is in the human heart, but it does not allow a positive postmortem connection to eternity.

Purgatory is also an attempt to extend the salvation opportunity beyond death. In Catholic doctrine, suffering purges us of our sin. It is a theological error to think that purging from sin and divine transformation occurs as a result of pain alone. The Holy Spirit inspired the author of Hebrews to write "how much more will the blood of Christ, who through the eternal spirit offered Himself without blemish to God, purify our conscience from dead works to serve the living God" (Heb. 9:14, NASB). In this case, it is biblical truth that pain and suffering does not eradicate sin; only the blood of Jesus washes away sin, which qualifies us for heaven. The decision to have our sins washed away by Jesus's blood has a time limit. Death ends that time. That is the weakness of purgatory.

Regarding the intermediate state, since Augustine, Christians have believed that the souls of those who die rest peacefully if they are Christian, or if the soul is afflicted, in the case of the damned, after death until the resurrection. Some theological traditions, including Protestants, Anabaptists, and Eastern Orthodox teach that the intermediate state is a disembodied foretaste of the final state. Those who die in Christ go into the presence of Christ (or the Bosom of Abraham) where they experience joy and rest waiting for the resurrection (Lk. 23:43). Those who are unrepentant will experience torment (perhaps in hell) as they await final condemnation on the Day of Judgment.[115] The main weakness of this doctrine is it offers no opportunity for salvation, just a precursor experience of the redeemed or the unbeliever before Judgment Day.[116]

None of the three attempts to escape death as the boundary for salvation and a positive relationship to eternity is able to fulfill the function for which it was created; that is, a positive relationship to the eternity that exists and has been placed in our heart can be accomplished only

---

115 Wikipedia, "Intermediate State, en.wikipedia.org/wiki/intermediate state....
116 Tillich, p. 418.

through the blood of Jesus Christ. Any attempt to positively relate to Father God, outside of the blood of Christ, will fail and destine the person to a postmortem eternity in hell temporarily and the lake of fire eternally. Any attempt at eternal life apart from the blood of Jesus places us "outside of Christ."

Not only are people outside of Christ when anything other than Jesus's blood is trusted for salvation, but there is also biblical truth that one can fall from grace (lose salvation) as a result of certain sins. These sins are identified by the Catholic Church and many Protestants as "mortal sins."[117] Writing to the Corinthian church, Paul clearly states grievous sins place the doer in danger of eternal judgment, but Paul also acknowledges these are former issues for them, for they had obviously repented of these sins by turning from them. They were now in a state

---

117 Based on I John 5:16–17, it is argued that there is a distinction between sins. "If anyone sees his brother committing a sin not leading to death, he shall ask and God will for him give life to those who commit sin not leading to death. There is a sin leading to death; I do not say that he should make request for this. All unrighteousness is sin, and there is a sin not leading to death."

Some biblical interpreters refer to the "sin unto death" as being the sin against the Holy Spirit, which will never be forgiven in this life or the next (Mt. 12:31, 32; Lk. 12:10), (John Gill, John Gill's Exposition of the Bible; read the I John 5:16, 17 commentary, www.biblestudytools.com/.../Ijohn-5-16.[17].html). However, a more widely held opinion, believed by the Catholic and some Protestant communities of faith, is that this passage reveals that there are mortal sins and venial sins. "A mortal sin removes your justification, and if you die with un-confessed mortal sin in your soul, you will be sent to hell. Venial sins do not destroy your justification and only reduce your rewards…" ("Mortal and Venial Sins," Bible.org/illustration/mortal-and-venal-sins).

The concepts of mortal and venial sins are essentially Roman Catholic. Evangelical Christians and Protestants may not be as familiar with these terms. As a working definition, mortal sin is a "sin causing spiritual death and merits eternal judgment but can be expiated by repentance." Venial sins (venial in Latin means lighter) merits temporal punishment and are expiated by repentance ("Does the Bible Teach Mortal and Venial sins," gotquestions.org).

of favor with God because God had blotted out their mortal sin by the blood of Jesus. They had been justified. (See I Cor. 6:9–11.)

Dating a New Testament letter of Paul's can at times be a difficult matter, however, assuming that Paul wrote I Corinthians in the spring of 57 CE, it may also be assumed that Paul wrote Ephesians while he was in prison five years later, in CE 62. In the letter to the Ephesians, Paul not only emphasized maintaining unity in the church (Eph. 4:1–3) but he also urged that the body of Christ be kept pure (Eph. 5:1–2). From Eph. 4:17–6:20, Paul gives practical instruction on how to live a holy, pure, and Christ-inspired lifestyle. In that section Paul again, five years after the first Corinthian correspondence, identifies mortal sin:

> For this you know with certainty, that no immoral or impure person or covetous man, who is an idolater, has an inheritance in the Kingdom of Christ and God." Let no one deceive you with empty words, for because of these things the wrath of God comes upon the sons of disobedience. Therefore do not be partakers with them, for you were formerly in darkness but now you are light in the Lord, walk as Children of Light. (Eph. 5:5–8, NASB)

Once again, mortal sin is clearly identified and its consequences emphasized. But, the mercy of the Lord is seen in that He has forgiven and turned from His wrath because these sinners committing those mortal sins repented.

Looking at the text, we see certainty on Paul's part. He writes "for this you know with certainty" (5:5). His words are very emphatic. In Ephesians 5:6 Paul again demonstrates his certainty about what he is writing when he says, "Let no one deceive you with empty words." He was certain that no immoral person or impure person or covetous man has any inheritance in the kingdom of Christ and God (Eph. 5:5). Those who commit such things will not only incur temporal judgment (Jn. 3:36; Rom. 1:18–32, 2:8–9, 9:22; Col. 3:6; I Thess. 2:16), they will be excluded from the kingdom of God. Paul is certain and does not want the Ephesians to be deceived; these sins will send a person to hell temporarily and ultimately he or she will be permanently consigned to the lake of fire.

Yet once again we see the love and mercy of God to extend forgiveness to those who repent of their mortal sin(s).[118] The point begs to be made; God reaches out to all humans, even those committing mortal sins, in agape love (self-sacrificing love; this type of love took Jesus to the cross) to reunite with those who have separated from Him. This is a universal truth (Rom. 5:5–8; Lk. 15:3–7, 15:8–10). Paul is very divulging about those sins that disqualify us from heaven, but Paul is also serious that any human who responds to God's consistent drawing love with repentance will be converted to Christian faith and discover that God's love will help him or her conquer all the ambiguities (all that is not of God) of life.[119]

The Apostle John emphasizes in the Revelation of Jesus Christ, just as Paul did in his epistles, that there are sins, when not repented of, that

---

118 The Ephesians had repented of their mortal sin, and in doing so were converted to Christianity. The rejection of the mortal sin and turning away from that mortal sin is called repentance. This repentance and faith in Christ resulted in conversion, and conversion affects all dimensions of human life. It is organic as well as psychological; it occurs under the predominance of the spirit and has a historical dimension. Repentance and conversion turns life around, as it did for the Ephesians who had been committing mortal sin, and Paul acknowledged their turnaround.

"The true nature of conversion is well expressed in the words denoting conversion in different languages. The word *Shubh* in Hebrew points to a turning around on one's way, especially in the social and political spheres. It points to a turning away from injustice toward justice, from inhumanity toward humanity, from idols to God. The Greek word *metanoia* implies the same idea but in relation to the mind, which changes from one direction to another, from the temporal to the eternal, from oneself to God. The Latin word *conversio* (in German *Be-kehrung*) unites the spatial image with the intellectual content. These words and the images they provoke suggest two elements: the negation of preceding direction of thought and action and the affirmation of the opposite direction"(Paul Tillich, *Systematic Theology*, vol. 3, pp. 219-220).

119 Paul Tillich, pp. 137, 138.

guarantee eternal damnation in the lake of Fire. In Revelation 21, after a vision of the new Jerusalem, John outlines the sad but guaranteed inheritance of those outside of Christ characterized as "fearful," "unbelieving," "abominable," "murderers," "whoremongers," "sorcerers," "idolaters," and "all liars" whose postmortem destiny is to be forever burned with fire and brimstone, which is the second death (Rev. 21:8). Those who are outside of Christ have their principal characteristics pictured in this list. (A similar list is found in 21:27, 22:15.) It is important to recognize that some of those saved from their sins by the blood of Jesus were guilty of offenses listed by John but had availed themselves in proper time (before death) of the grace of God through faith in Christ Jesus. Therefore they did not, nor will anyone else, experience the wrath of God, though mortal sin had been committed.[120]

CHAPTER CONCLUSION

This chapter explained what it means to be inside of Christ by defining the moment of new birth as the moment we received the august position of being "in Christ." This chapter also rehearsed the blessings of being "in Christ." Conversely, this chapter also explained what it means to be "outside of Christ," that is, being outside the salvation offered only by Father God through the blood of Jesus.

This chapter also reviewed and analyzed the attempts of three efforts to avoid death as being the moment to attain salvation from one's sins. These three efforts were reincarnation, purgatory, and the intermediate state.

Finally, this chapter identified mortal sins, sins that disqualify us from heaven, while noting God's absolute willingness to forgive those sins we ask and repent.

---

[120] Joseph F. Walvoord, *The Revelation of Jesus Christ*, Moody Press, Chicago, IL, 1966, pp. 316, 317.

Chapter Eight

The Love of God

Chapter Introduction

One of my favorite authors is Judson Cornwall. In his 1986 book, *Meeting God*, he identified that it is possible for people to tell the truth, yet their account may vary from other eyewitnesses. People see the same event differently.

Judson illustrates the point with a brief contrast between Peter and John. Both ministered with and for Jesus. They saw the same miracles and heard the same teachings, yet each assessed the circumstances differently. Peter saw the God-man, while John saw the nature of God in the man. Peter spoke of faith bringing us into an abundant "knowledge of our Lord Jesus Christ" (II Pet. 1:8), while John observed, "This is how we know love, Jesus laid down His life for us…" (I Jn. 3:16, NASB). Peter saw one perspective, the person of Christ, while John consistently referred to the light and love of Christ.[121]

After seven chapters of looking at the postmortem punishment of those who die outside of Christ, it is important that we understand that God does not want that for any of us, but it is His desire that we live in eternal sharing and discovery with Him. So we begin with a definition of God.

In his first epistle, John wrote, "God is Love" (I Jn. 4:8). The story is told of C. S. Lewis walking into a room where his academic colleagues

---

121 Judson Cornwall, *Meeting God*, Creation House, Altamonte Springs, FL, 1986, pp. 205-206. Chapter 10, titled "John Met a Loving God" will be referred to in this chapter detailing the love that God has for us, which is juxtaposed to the previous seven chapters of this book, which emphasize eternal punishment for those outside of Christ.

were trying to define God. The group was engaged in active debate and asked Lewis how to define God. Lewis answered that it was easy to define God; he said, "God is Love."

In the very next verse, I John 4:9, John was inspired by the Holy Spirit to write down his view of Jesus because it revealed God's love for us: "By this the love of God was manifested in us[a], that God has sent His[b] only begotten son into the world so that we might live through Him" (I Jn. 4:9, NASB; a) I John 4:9, or "in our case"; b) I John 4:9, or "unique, only one of His kind"; Bible Gateway, II Jn. 4:9 NASB footnotes, bible-gateway.com).

> As John reviewed it the secret of Christ's coming was two-fold. It declared God's love for us, and it demonstrated His willingness to show that love to us. Love seeks to express itself in gifts that will show forth its nature and that will best satisfy those it loves. God's moral love would have been forever unknown to us if He had not expressed it in a way that we could understand. [122]

John understood that, and that is why he followed his definition of God ("God is Love") with "...the love of God was manifested...that [He] sent his only begotten son...so that we might live through Him" (I Jn. 4:9). Through John's viewpoint, the Holy Spirit is revealing that the coming of Jesus was the supreme manifestation of divine love. There is no other manifestation of God's love that equals Him sending Jesus Christ, His only begotten son, into the world for the propitiation of our sins and to give us life (see Jn. 10:10, I Jn. 4:10). Cornwall cites Alexander McClaron's comments about God's love in volume 10 of his *Expositions of Holy Scripture* to further explain the revelation of God's love through Jesus: "Before Jesus Christ came into this world no one ever dreamt of saying 'God loves!' Some of the Old Testament Psalmists had glimpses of that truth and came pretty near expressing it. But among all the 'gods many and lords many,' there are lustful gods and beautiful gods, and

---

[122] Cornwall, *Meeting God*, p. 208.

idle gods, and fighting gods, and peaceful gods, but not one of whom worshippers said 'He loves!' 'God Loves' is the greatest thing that can be said by lips."

This chapter will provide an overview of the reality of hell and the lake of fire through the lens that God loves us and does not want us to choose not coming to Him as an option. God's desire is that we dwell with Him, in everlasting joy and ever unfolding revelation (I Thess. 5:9–11; Rev. 2:10).

AGAPE: EXTENDING REUNION TO THE SEPARATED

The Greek word "agape," often translated "unconditional love," is one of the *Koine* (everyday speech) Greek words translated into English as "love." It is used in Christianity to describe the self-sacrificing love that God has for us. Whereas the word "faith" has a predominately religious meaning, the word "love" is so equivocal (possibility of several different meanings) that the Holy Spirit had to give us the word "agape" to describe the love God has for each of us.

In his book, *Those Who Love Him,* Basilea Schlink helped to illustrate agape love, the self-sacrificing love. He wrote: "Yet behold Him again, this King and Lord! See Him humble and lowly. He leaves the glory of heaven, He come to sons of men, to sinners. They do not want Him, and they will not receive Him. Yet, He comes. They hated Him in return. Yet He loves them still. In the end they torture Him to death. They deride and mock. Then they nail Him to a cross. Yet toward them are words of love and compassion. He is a Foolish love. A spendthrift love that lavishes love upon those who trample Him under Foot."[123] Agape love is the self-sacrificing form of love that God has for people,

---

123 Cornwall, *Meeting God*, p. 212.

which caused God to send Jesus to come to the earth to die on a cross for our sins (Rom. 5:8, I Jn. 4:10).[124]

Knowing God's love for each and every human being who has ever lived, we can discern His heart of mercy. When Job called for God to separate the righteous from the unrighteous in Sheol (Job lived ca. 2000 BCE) in Job 21:23–26, the reader is not cognizant of God's broken heart for those who are unrighteous (also known as the wicked and those outside of Christ). Ezekiel, writing fourteen hundred years after Job, details God's brokenness over the unrighteous.

> "Do I have any pleasure in the death of the wicked," declares the Lord God, "rather than that he should turn from his ways and live?" (Ezekiel 18:23, NASB)

> Say to them, "As I live," declares the Lord God, "I take no pleasure in the death of the wicked, but rather that the wicked turn from his way and live. Turn back, turn back, from your evil ways!" (Ezekiel 33:11)

From Adam and Eve's expulsion from Eden until the beginning of Jesus's ministry, few people had thought of God as loving. God was seen as austere, judgmental, powerful, and holy but not as loving.[125] Looking back with the revelation of God's heart, we can see that He wanted no one to enter Sheol as unrighteous, nor does Father God want that today. God took no pleasure in the judgments upon the generation of Noah (Gen. 6–9), the destruction of the five cities of the plain including Sodom and Gomorrah (Gen. 18,19), the death of Aaron's two sons, (Lev. 10:1–2),

---

124 God has always had agape love for humankind, from Adam forward. We know this by the testimony about Jesus, who is the perfect revelation of the Father (Heb. 3:1; Jn. 10:30, 14:9). "Jesus Christ is the same yesterday, today, and forever" (Heb. 13:8, NASB). Additionally, through Malachi's writings, God the Father proclaims that He does not change (see Malachi 3:6).

125 Cornwall, *Meeting God*, pp. 212, 213.

the death of Korah, Dathan, and Abiram, and Dathan's and Abiram's families (Num. 16), and on it goes. So from the perspective of humans, we see the judgment side of God, but from God's perspective it was not what he wanted for those listed or for the many others that were not listed.

For those of us who live today, because we know God is love, we can be sure that Him taking pleasure in the death of the unrighteous person is not in His nature. It never has been.

By the sending of His son, Jesus, it is abundantly certain that God loves sinners. Even those that have committed mortal sins God will forgive and write their names in the book of life. In I Corinthians 6:9–11, Paul lists mortal sins in verses 9 and 10, but in verse 11, Paul reports that some of them had turned from the mortal sin to Jesus's salvation, and now they are justified before God and will receive eternal life, not eternal postmortem judgment in hell and the lake of fire. The same is true in Ephesians 5:5–8 and Revelation 21:7–8, except in this passage John begins with the promise that whoever overcomes the sins He is about to list, which characterize the unrighteous, they will inherit all things, obviously including eternal life.

We have a loving God who takes no pleasure when someone chooses not to live with Him through all of eternity and completes life in that stance. To demonstrate His absolute disinterest in a person dying outside of Christ, God sent Jesus, in a supreme act of love, to die on the cross. It is important to understand that Jesus did not die to make God love us; God gave His son to die because He loves us. Whenever we are tempted to doubt God's love for us, we need only to remind ourselves of Calvary (from the Greek) or Golgotha (from the Hebrew). John wrote "…He loved us and send His son to be a propitiation (to make favorable) for our sins" (I Jn. 4:10, NASB).

The agape of God (the love of God) is that ecstatic divine love that urges a reunion between Him and whoever has been separated from Him. It applies to all of us without exception. All that has to be done to bring about the reunion is for us to confess our sins to the Lord Jesus (the one who died for our sins). Then demonstrate our belief that He has been resurrected by cooperating with the Holy Spirit as He reorders our life to the things of God (see Romans 10:9).

SATAN BLURS THE AGAPE OF GOD

Peter wrote in his first epistle to the believers, "Be of sober spirit, be on the alert. Your adversary, the devil, prowls around like a roaring lion, seeking someone to devour" (I Pet. 5:8, NASB). Peter was clear: our enemy is the devil, also called Satan. His name was Lucifer in heaven, but after being cast out, he was called by his nicknames:

1) "Accuser" (Revelation 12:10)
2) "Dragon" (Revelation 12:7)
3) "Serpent" (Revelation 12:9)
4) "Devil" (Matthew 4:1)
5) "Satan" (Mark 8:33)[126]

Satan is a real personality.[127] He is mentioned fifty-five times in forty-nine separate verses, and in each of these he is viewed as a person. There is no hint that Satan is a thought or an imaginary influence in the world. From Genesis to Revelation, the Bible acknowledges that Satan is as real as Michael or Gabriel. Satan does not have a human body; he

---

126 Cornwall, *Back to Basics*, pp. 163, 164.

127 This is a list of seven statements from the Bible that prove Satan is a real personality, a real being:
    a. Jesus taught that Satan was real (Lk. 10:18).
    b. Jesus waged war with Satan (Lk. 13:16).
    c. Jesus dealt with Satan as a being (Mt. 4:1–11).
    d. Personal statements are made to Satan (Isa. 14:12–15).
    e. Personal singular pronouns are used of Satan (Mt. 4:7–11).
    f. Personal descriptions are given of Satan (Ezk. 28:11–19).
    g. Personal acts are attributed to Satan (Mt. 4:5).

For further statements refer to Cornwall, *Back to Basics*, "The Basics of Our Enemy," pp. 164, 165.

has the spiritual body of an angel, which makes him invisible unless he elects to display himself.

As to where Satan came from, we have scriptural insight. Ezekiel 28:12–19 explains his title, his appearance, and the glory he formerly enjoyed. Ezekiel calls him the "anointed Cherub that covers" (Ezk. 28:14). Cherubim (cherub is singular for cherubim) occupy a unique position:

> The Cherubim are symbolic of God's holy presence and His unapproachable majesty…God has placed Cherubim to guard the way to the tree of life. Also when Moses made the mercy seat and placed it into the Tabernacle's Holy of Holies, God's glory came and dwelt between the Cherubim. They covered the mercy seat with their wings. Through Ezekiel, we see that Satan was a cherub and his position was to guard the very throne of God. His position was that of protecting the Holiness of God. Satan had the highest of all positions, a position which he despised and lost. We have here in Ezekiel a picture of the highest of God's creatures, perfect in wisdom, beautiful beyond description, a musician…but, this creation, with all of these wonderful attributes also had a free will. One day, God says to this marvelous creature, "iniquity was found in you." (Ezekiel 28:15)[128]

That iniquity caused Satan and one-third of the angels to be cast out of heaven (though Satan himself still has access to heaven), and that created a jealousy and hatred of humankind because humankind is loved by God. Satan is antagonistic to God and to goodness, which God prizes: "The worldwide and age-long works of Satan are to be traced to one predominant motive. He hates both God and man and all that is in him lies

---

128 Read the KJB, "Why Was Satan Called 'The Anointed Cherub that Covereth?,'" answers.yahoo.com/questions/index?qid…

to defeat God's plan of grace and to establish and maintain a Kingdom of evil in the seduction and rule of mankind."[129]

Satan's chief power is his ability to deceive; however, the Bible also teaches that man participates in the process of his own deception. "He is deceived only because he ceases to love the truth and comes first to love and then to believe a lie (II Cor. 1:10)…The whole power of sin, at least in its beginning, consists in the sway of the fundamental falsehood that any good is really attainable by wrongdoing."[130] Satan works through deception to disqualify people from living eternally with God; he works to see that what God loves (human beings) is cast downward into hell and ultimately into the eternal lake of fire. He will use persons and institutions to deceive. The Scripture clearly indicates "that Satan is the instigator of that spirit of lawlessness which exhibits itself as hatred both of the truth and right, and which has operated so widely and so disastrously in human life."[131]

In his deceptions, Satan blurs the agape love of God. By his deceptions he pictures God as unfeeling, uncaring, impossible to please, impatient with humanity, and anxious to judge and take joy from life. But those are his deceptions. And Satan has this goal: to take as many as he can to the place where they are separated from God, take humanity down to the place where he will ultimately be—hell and then the lake of fire.

Accepting the Agape Love of God Brings Us up Where We Belong

It has been said that the love of God lifts us from the "guttermost to the uttermost." John wrote, "By this the love of God was manifested in us, that God has sent His only begotten son into the world so that we

---

129 James Orr, *The International Standard Bible Encyclopedia*, vol. 5, "Satan," WMB. Eerdmans Publishing Co., Grand Rapids, MI, p. 2694.

130 Ibid., p. 2694.

131 Ibid., p. 2694.

might live through Him" (I Jn. 4:9, NASB). Scholars tell us that God's love was manifested "in us," so it is God not just displaying His love but actually living in us; thus the believer lives out of the power of God's love for all to observe.

God has chosen to share His very nature with us, and He who is love is also life. John made this clear when he wrote "God has given us eternal life, and this life is in His Son. He who has the Son has life; he who does not have the Son of God does not have life" (I Jn. 5:11, 12, NASB).

Jesus, who came as an expression of God's agape love, is God's channel of divine life. The life that Adam lost in Eden has been restored in Jesus. Too, after coming to Jesus, we are lifted up to the esteemed place of being the child of God. In great joy, his quill moving excitedly over the parchment, John writes: "See how great a love the Father hath bestowed on us, that we would be called Children of God...Beloved now we are the Children of God..." (I Jn. 3:1, 2, NASB). By accepting the agape love of God, we are infused with the character of Jesus, for He lives in us through the Holy Spirit; old things in our life pass away, and the new comes forth. We have been lifted up in this life to eternal meaning and in the next-to-eternal togetherness with God, all because we made Jesus the Lord of our lives.[132]

Chapter Conclusion

To avoid hell and the lake of fire, Jesus is the answer. He is the only answer; there is no other. God's "so great salvation" (Heb. 2:3, NASB) is Jesus Christ. Peter explicitly stated, in no uncertain terms, to the rulers of Israel, "And there is salvation in no one else; for there is no other name under Heaven that has been given among men by which we must be saved" (Acts 4:12, NASB).

Gabriel, the angel of the incarnation, the angel who stands before God (Lk. 1.9), instructed Joseph, "...you shall call His name Jesus, for He will save His people from their sins" (Mt. 1:21, NASB). Jesus is the savior,

---

132 Cornwall, *Meeting God*, pp. 218-219.

and through Him alone can anyone be saved from the consequences of their sin, be saved from the unfathomable punishments of hell and the lake of fire. None of us can save ourselves; we can only accept what God has provided by the cross of Jesus Christ, where His shed blood washes away all sin (I Jn. 1:7; Mt 26:26–28; Eph. 2:12; Heb. 13:12; Rev. 1:5).[133]

As I conclude this study on hell, which extended to the lake of fire (the postmortem judgment of God upon those who conclude this life outside of Christ) , I pray that this has been a thought provoking overview of the wrath to come. For those outside of Christ's salvation I hope that earnest and strong consideration will be given to fleeing the coming wrath. For those in-Christ I hope there is renewed interest in living a vibrant Christian life and a zeal to warn others to flee the wrath to come.

---

133 Cornwall, *Back to Basics*, pp. 27-30.

Bibliography

- Alcon, Randy, "Do Infants Go to Heaven when They Die?," www.epm.org.
- Barker, Kenneth, *Zondervan NIV Study Bible*, Zondervan, Grand Rapids, MI, 2002.
- Barnes Notes, bibleapps.com.
- Barth, Karl, *Church Dogmatics*, vol. 4, Hendrickson Publishers, Peabody, MA.
- Bernstein, Alan, *The Formation of Hell*, Cornell University Press, Ithaca, NY, 1993.
- Cabal, Ted, *The Apologetics Study Bible*, Holman Bible Publishers, Nashville, TN, 2007.
- "Charts for Sheol, Hades, Gehenna, and Tartarus," www.what-the-hell-is-hell.com,
- "Churches Ineffective," bible.org.
- "Common Era," Simple Wikipedia.org.
- Cornwall, Judson, *Back to Basics*, Cerdic Chivers Ltd., Brentwood, Essex, England, 1994.
- Cornwall, Judson, *Meeting God*, Creation House, Altamonte Springs, FL, 1986.
- Cornwall, Judson, *The Best of Judson Cornwall*, Bridge Publishing Inc., South Plainfield, NJ, 1992.
- Cornwall, Judson, *Incense and Insurrection*, Destiny Publishers Inc., Shippensburg, PA, 1995.
- Cross, F. L., *The Oxford Dictionary of the Christian Church*, Oxford University Press, London, England.
- "Cyprian," Wikipedia.org.

- Dake, Finnish Jennings, *Dake's Annotated Reference Bible*, Dake Bible Sales Inc., Lawrenceville, GA, 2004.

- Edwards, Jonathan, "Sinners in the Hands of an Angry God," Voiceofdemocracy.umd.edu.

- *Full Life Study Bible*, NIV, Zondervan Corp., Grand Rapids, MI, 2004.

- Garrison, Greg, *USA Today*, "Many Americans Don't Believe in Hell, But What about the Pastors?" 30.usatoday.com, August 1, 2009.

- Gill, John, "Exposition of the Bible," www.biblestudytools.com.

- Gospel of John, www.theopedia.com.

- Gromacki, Robert, *New Testament Survey*, Baker Book House, Grand Rapids, MI, 1974.

- Harrison, R. K., *The Book of Job*, New International Commentary, Eerdmaus, Grand Rapids, MI, 1988.

- Hash, Ronald, "Is There Salvation after Death?," www.equip.org.

- "Hell, the Wise Avoid," bibleapps.com.

- Hodge, A. A., *Popular Lectures on Theological Themes*, Presbyterian Board of Publications, Philadelphia, PA, 1887.

- Hoodman, Michael, "Book of Romans," www.gotquestions.org.

- "How Many Americans Attend Church Each Week," thegospelcoalition.org, March 1, 2007.

- "How Many Covenants Are There?," christeternalchristianchurch.com.

- "How Was the Book of Job Written," answers.yahoo.com.

- Jennings, Jack, "Proportion of U.S. Students in Private Schools is 10 Percent and Declining," www.huffingtonpost.com, March 18, 2014.

- Johnson, Greg, "God Rescues the Righteous," www.lovinggodfellowship.org

- Kennedy, James, Dr., *Why I Believe*, Word Publishing, Dallas, TX, 1980.

- Liberty University Online, "Hell, Sheol, Hades, Gehenna, and Tartarus Explained," http://www.scribd.com/doc/22685585/Hell-Sheol-Hades-Gehenna-and-Tartarus-explained

- *Life Application Study Bible*, Tyndale House Publishers Inc., Wheaton, IL, 1996.

- Morrison, James, L., "Some Thoughts about the Judgment of God," Scripture insights.com.

- "Mortal and Venial Sins," Bible.org.

- New Living Translation, biblehub.com.

- Orr, James, "Sheol," *International Standard Bible Encyclopedia*, Grand Rapids, MI, 1980.

- Preaching Today, "Top Ten Sermons of 2011," preachingtoday.com.

- "Pulpit Commentary Reference," biblehub.com/2 Peter/2-4.htm.

- Quinn, John, "The Meaning of Being 'In-Christ,'" www.bradleychurchofchrist.com.

- "Reincarnation Facts and Resources," www.datahookup.com.

- Richardson, Grant C., "Verse by Verse Commentary," versebyversecommentary.com.

- Rittenbaugh, John W., Bible Tools, "Satan" and "After Pentecost, Then What?" (Forerunner Commentary), BibleTools.com, undated.

- Rosenblatt, Roger, "What Really Mattered?," *Time* magazine, 50th anniversary edition, October, 1983.

- Schaeffer, Francis, *The Complete Works of Francis Schaeffer, A Christian Worldview*, vol. 4, *The Great Evangelical Disaster*, Crossway Books, Westchester, IL, 1982.

- Seeley, Bethany, "Why Is John's Gospel Different from the Synoptic Gospels?," www.ehow.com/info.8475770_johns-gospel-different-synopic-gospels.html.

- Tabor, James, "What the Bible Says about Death, Afterlife and the Future," clas-pagesunce.edu.

- "The Aaronic Priesthood—A Biblical Analysis," help4ldrs.com/pwtu/PWTU chapter14.pdf.

- *The Preacher's Outline and Sermon Bible*, Leadership Ministries Worldwide, Chattanooga, TN, vol. 3, 1998.

- Towner, Wayne, "The Abrahamic Covenant," bibletrack.org.

- Tillich, Paul, *Systematic Theology*, The University of Chicago Press, Chicago, IL.

- Walvoord, Joseph, and Zuck, Roy B., *The Bible Knowledge Commentary*, Victor Books, Wheaton, IL, 1983.

- Walvoord, Joseph F., *The Revelation of Jesus Christ*, Moody Press, Chicago, IL, 1966.

- "What Is the First Resurrection? What Is the Second Resurrection?," www.gotquestions.org.

- "Why Is Satan Called the Anointed Cherub that Covereth?," answers.yahoo.com.

-Wilkerson, David, "God Will Restore Your Wasted Years!," missionventureministries.wordpress.com/2011.12/06/god….

- "24 Percent of Americans Believe in Reincarnation," www.prokerala.com.

Made in United States
Orlando, FL
15 July 2022